THE WEST COAST
BED &
BREAKFAST
GUIDE

Breakfast at the Carter House, Eureka, California

THE WEST COAST
BED &
BREAKFAST
GUIDE
CALIFORNIA – OREGON
WASHINGTON

BY COURTIA WORTH AND TERRY BERGER

Photographs by Will Faller

DESIGNED AND PRODUCED BY
ROBERT R. REID
AND
TERRY BERGER

SIMON AND SCHUSTER
NEW YORK

FRONT COVER PHOTOGRAPH:
  Guest House Bed & Breakfast, Whidbey Island, Washington
FRONTISPIECE PHOTOGRAPH:
  Starrett House Inn, Port Townsend, Washington

Editorial assistance by Amelia Weiss
  and Roberta Gardner
Maps by Anthony St. Aubyn

A Robert Reid/Terry Berger production
Typeset in Bodoni Book by Monotype Composition Company, Baltimore
Printed and bound by Mandarin Offset Marketing (H.K.) Ltd.

1 2 3 4 5 6 7 8 9 10

Library of Congress Cataloging in Publication Data

Worth, Courtia.
    The West Coast bed & breakfast guide.

    1. Hotels, taverns, etc.—California—Directories.
2. Hotels, taverns, etc.—Oregon—Directories.
3. Hotels, taverns, etc.—Washington (State)—
Directories.   I. Berger, Terry.   II. Title: West Coast
bed and breakfast guide.
TX907.W694 1984   647'.9479   84-10682

CONTENTS

Arcata
Eureka
Ferndale

NORTHERN
CALIFORNIA

Westport

Elk

Boonville
Gualala

WINE COUNTRY

Cloverdale
Geyserville
Healdsburg
St. Helena
Sonoma
Napa

Grass Valley
Colfax
Auburn

Placerville

Sutter Creek

GOLD COUNTRY

Murphys
Tuolumne

Inverness

Muir Beach

Berkeley

SAN FRANCISCO

Davenport
Santa Cruz
Aptos

Pacific Grove

MONTEREY

Monterey
Carmel

Cambria
Templeton
San Luis Obispo
Arroyo Grande

SOUTHERN
CALIFORNIA

Santa Barbara

North Hollywood
Pasadena

Santa Monica
Venice
LOS ANGELES

Newport Beach

Vista
Julian

Del Mar
SAN DIEGO

*NOTE: all the cities and towns on this map contain
the bed and breakfasts described in this book.*

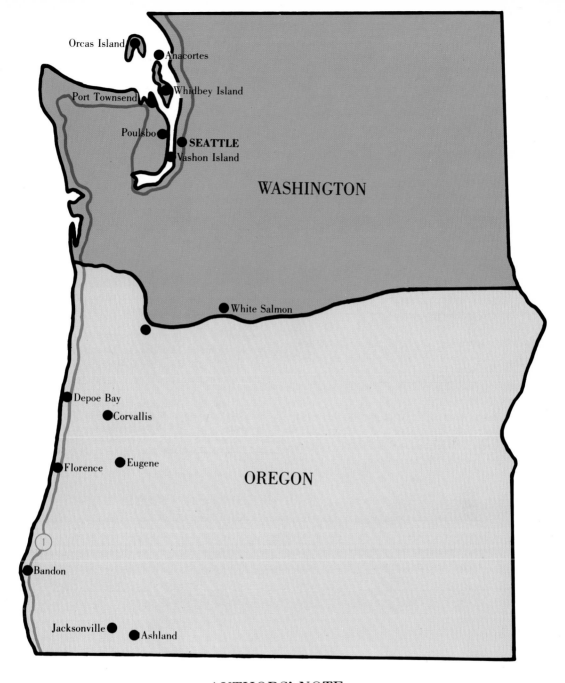

AUTHORS' NOTE

Americans are quickly discovering the charm, adventure, romance, good value, and personal attention that typify bed and breakfast travel. Opportunities to form new friendships and to find camaraderie with both hosts and guests present themselves in a setting of relaxed intimacy.

To make a visit most successful, we offer the following tips:

• Cancellations are difficult for places with a limited number of guest rooms.

• If your arrival will be delayed, call your host just as you would a friend who was expecting you.

• Adhere to the policy regarding smoking, children, and pets.

• Remember that you are in someone's home, and that mutual kindness and respect and general consideration will enhance the bed and breakfast experience.

SOUTHERN CALIFORNIA

THE COTTAGE

Cottage hideaway in San Diego

A stroll down a walkway beside the main house leads to a secluded hideaway with several fruit trees framing the doorway. Lovingly decorated with turn-of-the-century furnishings, the house boasts an oak pump organ that works, a three-foot-high coffee grinder that promises to produce a fine blend, and a potbellied wood-burning stove that takes the chill out of the morning air.

A tap on your door in the morning and breakfast appears: a tray of steaming hot bread, fresh fruit, and coffee or tea, along with a morning paper. It is easy to grow fond of this intimate, self-contained house, with bedroom, sitting room, kitchen, small dining area, and private bath. Within walking

Fresh fruit and nuts await guests.

distance of shops and restaurants, five minutes by car from the San Diego Zoo and Balboa Park, and thirty minutes from Mexico, you are well located to make the most of your stay.

THE COTTAGE, P.O. Box 3292, San Diego, CA 92103; (619) 299-1564; Carol and Robert Emerick, hosts. One cottage with a king-size bed in bedroom and a single bed in living room. Rates: single $40, double $45, triple $50. Includes generous continental breakfast. No pets; no credit cards; smoking permitted.

DIRECTIONS: contact hosts.

Antiques, including a working pump organ, furnish the Cottage.

A classic wood stove warms the lobby, where breakfast is served.

JULIAN HOTEL

Well-worn character

In the 1870s the first discoveries of gold were made a few hundred yards from the Julian Hotel, which stands today as the sole surviving hostelry to have lived through the glory of the mining boom. Each of the many rooms off the long hallways retains the full flavor of the frontier, and one senses there haven't been a great many changes since the original guests polished their pistols here. Well-worn character prevails over fancy frills, and the visitor should not object to the shared "necessary rooms for ladies and gentlemen" down the hall.

Breakfast is served on card tables set up in the lobby across from the wood-burning stove. And one can browse through the original guest registers dating back a hundred years to the time when the hotel was built by freed slaves.

While in this classic, false-front western town, you might enjoy the Wildflower Festival in the spring, or the Banjo and Fiddle Festival in the fall. Whatever the time of year, the apple pie is a treat to be considered seriously at any of the local restaurants.

JULIAN HOTEL, P.O. Box 856, Julian, CA 92036; (619) 765-0201; Steve and Gig Ballinger, owners; Dee Baker, manager. Sixteen rooms, shared and private baths, and a Honeymoon Cottage. Open all year, closed every Tuesday. Rates: weeknights $18 to $55; weekends $23 to $70. Includes full breakfast. Children under sixteen during week; no pets; no credit cards; smoking permitted.

DIRECTIONS: from L.A. take I-5 south to Rte. 78 east through Escondido to Julian (2½ hrs.). From San Diego, take I-8 east to Rte. 79 north to Julian (1¾ hrs.).

The bungalow overlooks town and tides.

SHADOW MOUNTAIN RANCH

Tree house under the stars

If you have a touch of Peter Pan in your soul, there is a Tree-House Suite at Shadow Mountain Ranch to fulfill your dreams. Ingeniously designed and built by owners Jim and Loretta Ketcherside, the tree house is easily accessible and includes a sitting area, bedside table, lamp, and even a place to hang your clothes. Extremely popular, it is wise to book in advance. If sleeping under the stars is not what you had in mind, several more traditional alternatives are available in the ranch house and a bunk house.

A full ranch breakfast is served daily, and includes juice, a fruit platter, hot cereal, fresh eggs, pancakes, sausage, and candy sticks.

This eight-acre working ranch is fourteen years old, and guests can help out with feeding the cattle, horses, chickens, and geese, or just relax in the spa, shoot a game of pool, or, as the owner puts it, "just enjoy lots of rocking-chair time."

SHADOW MOUNTAIN RANCH, 2771 Frisius Road, P.O. Box 791, Julian, CA 92036; (619) 765-0323. Jim & Loretta Ketcherside, hosts. Four rooms, plus tree house; three baths, all shared. Rates: $50.00, single or double. Full ranch breakfast. No children or pets; no smoking; no credit cards.

DIRECTIONS: from L.A. Take I-5 to Rte. 78 through Escondido. One mile before Julian there is a Methodist Church on the left and a sign for Pine Hills Lodge. Turn right onto Pine Hills Road. Go 2½ miles and take a left onto Frisius Road; entrance to the ranch is on the right. From San Diego take I-8 to Rte. 79 north through Julian one mile to the Methodist Church as above.

Left, the Tree House, where the climb is worthwhile.

ROCK HAUS

Spectacular sunsets

As soon as you step onto the enclosed veranda and take in its panoramic view of the ocean, you'll know you have stopped at a special place. Rock Haus is inviting for breakfast and awesome at sunset, and the day can be spent walking on the beach, browsing through the fancy shops, or cheering on your favorite Thoroughbred at the Del Mar Racetrack.

This landmark 1910 bungalow-style house has a large and welcoming living room, where wine is served from the host's personal wine cellar. Rooms named Whale Watch, Wicker Garden, and Court Room, among others, have been meticulously decorated, each with individual charm and character.

ROCK HAUS, 410 15th Street, Del Mar, CA 92014; (619) 481 3764; Carol & Tom Hauser, hosts. Eight rooms, two with private bath and separate entry on ground floor; remaining six rooms upstairs share three well-located bathrooms, two with tile showers and third with tub. Rates: $60 to $85, slightly less during the week. Includes continental breakfast and wine in the evening. Visa/MasterCard; no children, pets, or smoking. Situated in the heart of Del Mar village; shops & beach are just a short walk away.

DIRECTIONS: from I-5 exit at Via de la Valle and head west to Jimmy Durante Blvd. Take a left and feed into US-101. Take a left on 15th Street.

BITTERSWEET HILL.

Terraced privacy

Convenient to the beach, and with San Diego only twenty-five minutes away in one direction, Mexico forty-five minutes in the other, this California-Spanish home is built on a hill in a residential community. The elegance of the open, expansive layout and the terraced privacy come as no surprise, for this is the five-hundredth house your host has built.

The furnishings are particularly interesting: museum-quality Oriental antiques collected over a lifetime; contemporary pottery; and original German beer steins from pre-World War I days.

Here you can rest assured of being catered to graciously and with a generous spirit, for your hosts have perfected the art of welcoming guests. They will help you plan your day, select a restaurant, and see to it that your stay in Vista is memorable. You can luxuriate in the Jacuzzi or swim in the pool; you should also inquire about the availability of the thirty-eight-foot Downeast cutter.

BITTERSWEET HILL, Vista, CA. Spanish spoken. Two rooms with private baths plus third for teenage overflow. One room has twin beds with bath attached, other room has double bed with bath across hall. Rates: single $40, double $45, triple $50. Includes continental breakfast served on outside terrace. Children welcome; no pets; smoking permitted. Siamese cat in residence. Wild animal farm, tennis, golf nearby. *Represented by Carolyn's Bed & Breakfast Homes in San Diego.*

Left, in California, a poolside breakfast is de rigeur. Above, the botanical gardens in San Diego's Balboa Park.

DORYMAN'S INN

Total luxury at Newport Beach

It is immediately apparent that no expense or comfort was spared in the execution of this extraordinary bed and breakfast. As you step off the street into a small vestibule, a receding oak door exposes an expansive gold leaf mirror, luminous brass railing, quartersawed wainscoting, silk wallpaper, and rich wool carpeting. You have just stepped into the elevator at Doryman's Inn.

Upon arriving at the second floor, you are ushered along a skylighted hallway to one of the opulent rooms. Appointments include Italian mar- ble fireplaces, luxurious window seats, antique furnishings, and artwork collected from all over the world.

The effort to please is apparent, whether you take the guest room with the sitting area, balcony, four-poster, conference table, and marble Jacuzzi, or the room with the ocean view and the rosette pleated canopy. One-way glass has been installed in all of the windows to ensure total privacy, walls are insulated, and doors are two-and-a-half-inches of solid oak. Bedside controls raise or lower gas-fueled fireplaces that glow in all the rooms, and each of the marble bathrooms has a fern-filled skylight, sunken tub, and telephone.

A buffet-style full breakfast is served in the parlor and may be eaten there or elsewhere. Other features of this 1921 landmark building include a redwood sun deck and Jacuzzi for eight on top of the complex, and Rex's fine restaurant on the ground floor. As if that weren't enough, Doryman's is located right at the beach and boardwalk of Newport Pier.

DORYMAN'S INN, 2102 W. Ocean Front, Newport Beach, CA 92663; (714) 675-7300; Mr. and Mrs. Richard Lawrence, owners; Carman Barbero, Julian Rigotti, David Stephens, hosts. French and Italian spoken. Ten rooms with private baths. Rates: $120 to $225. Includes a full breakfast. No children; no pets; Visa/ MasterCard/American Express.
DIRECTIONS: located at the base of Newport Pier.

Friendly service at the front desk.

Two of the luxurious guest rooms at Doryman's Inn.

CASA ALMA

A whitewashed oasis of folk art

High, whitewashed walls surrounding homes always pique one's curiosity. Upon entering the courtyard of this Mediterranean villa, you can be assured of making intriguing discoveries.

For years the owners of Casa Alma have collected folk art and crafts from Central and South America. Adorning the living room are large, vibrantly colored yarn paintings by the Huichol Indians, and elaborate weavings hang throughout the house. Tin figurines, symbolic dolls, and pottery are casually displayed, and if you are at all interested in anthropology, the origin and meaning of each piece will be happily explained.

Hardly a modest affair, Casa Alma has two dining rooms, a television room, a large living room, and an entirely separate guest wing. At the same time guests are afforded the opportunity for privacy, they are offered all the warmth, comfort, and amenities of a private home.

Outdoors, a pool nestled amid flowers and blooming cactus is the center of an enchanting garden. The setting is so idyllic, in fact, that one is startled to be reminded that this home is located across from Will Rogers State Beach, one of California's most popular beaches, and a short way from Los Angeles.

CASA ALMA, Santa Monica, CA. Spanish spoken. Four rooms, each with connecting bath shared with one other room. Spanish décor with sitting area and writing desk in each room. Rates: $65 double. Includes American or continental breakfast. Dog Lucky and cat Titi in residence. Smoking permitted. *Represented by Bed & Breakfast International.*

Hosts Alma and Joe at the hacienda entrance. Right, the grand entrance hall to Casa Alma.

LA MAIDA HOUSE

North Hollywood Mediterranean villa

Italian artisans, brought here in the 1920s, adorned this seven-thousand-square-foot Sicilian mansion with ironwork, woodwork, marble, and fountains. Built on a grand scale, it is a villa not unlike those found on the Mediterranean.

The splendor of magnolia trees, blooming orchids, and three hundred varieties of roses can be viewed from the stained-glass-covered solarium, while the grace of a former era is reflected in the expansive living room and a dining room that seats thirty-four. There are several casual niches for relaxing, among them a multitiered couch in the game room and an upstairs porch for intimate dining.

The rooms, filled with fresh flowers from La Maida's gardens, are airy and elegant. An especially glorious one, in the main house, is the Cipresso Suite, with a white-canopied four-poster bed, wicker chaise, mirrored dressing room, and large blue-tiled bathroom. Downstairs the sun pours through white lace curtains, creating beautiful shadows at arched windows. Adding to the warmth are the stained-glass windows designed and made by Megan Timothy, La Maida's hostess.

The windows only hint at Megan's artistry, for in addition to working with clay, stone, and fabric, she is a highly skilled cook. A beautifully presented continental breakfast is an introduction to epicurean dinners that Megan can arrange and prepare for you and your guests.

LA MAIDA HOUSE, 11159 La Maida Street, North Hollywood, CA 91601; (818) 769-3857; Megan Timothy, hostess. Three rooms in main house; four in annexed houses. Several with private entrances. Rates: $70 to $105. Includes generous continental breakfast. Phone and TV provided on request. Business and social affairs arranged. No children under sixteen; no pets; smoking permitted only in the garden; no credit cards. A flock of elegant chickens provides fresh eggs.

DIRECTIONS: from Hollywood Frwy 170, exit at Tujunga Blvd, proceed under overpass, take a right on Camarillo Street, and proceed three blocks. Turn left onto Bellflower. Go one block to La Maida; the house is on the corner.

Left, the king-sized redwood, tile, and stained-glass bathroom of the Cipresso Suite. Above, extra-long beds in the Fontana Room.

A beautifully restored Craftsman bungalow.

SALISBURY HOUSE

Country charm in Los Angeles

A meticulous arrangement of porcelain dolls, family photographs, Victorian ornaments, baskets of flowers, and sparkling crystal surround you when you enter this 1910 craftsman-style house. Owners Kathleen Salisbury and her husband Bill have created this dream-come-true, magical oasis of warmth and laughter—quite unexpectedly in the heart of Los Angeles. Each guest room has its own personality, with turn-of-the-century memorabilia, stuffed animals, and assortments of sachets, potpourris, talcums, fragrant sprays, candles, and candies, carefully chosen to complement the color-coordinated décor. The top floor, with its pitched roof and freestanding tub, has its own special charm.

Piping hot Amaretto coffee appears in the morning in a silver urn on the mahogany sideboard. Elegant as the house may appear, you are welcome to wear your robe down to enjoy the Salisbury's full, hearty breakfast.

SALISBURY HOUSE, 2273 West 20th Street, Los Angeles, CA 90018; (213) 737-7817; Kathleen Salisbury, hostess. Five rooms, three with private bath. Rates: $45 to $55. Includes full breakfast and complimentary wine. No children under twelve; no pets; smoking permitted. Located downtown, near El Cholo, L.A.'s oldest Mexican restaurant.

DIRECTIONS: from Santa Monica Freeway (exit 10), go north on Western Avenue, turn left on 20th St.

The Attic Suite offers all the amenities.

The soft light of the seashore glows in Cora's Corner guest room.

VENICE BEACH HOUSE

Romantic lodgings near the beach

This recently restored house by the sea is a survivor of the splendid era of expansive two-story shingled beach houses, shaded verandas, and a more carefree way of life. Whether it is the breeze off the ocean, just steps away, or the genuine southern hospitality of the hostesses, mother and daughter, one feels privileged to have discovered the Venice Beach House.

Sophisticated décor enhances the romantic quality of this 1911 house, with its extensive use of wool wall coverings. The mood shifts from the contemporary elegance of the Pier Suite, a cool gray accented with rose, to Cora's Corner, a hot pink and white wicker room with a four-poster bed. The room named after town father Abbott Kinney is covered in Scottish plaid wool, hunter green carpet, and dark wainscoting.

An additional pleasure is bathing side by side in a large, lush bathroom in claw-foot tubs, or enjoying the double Jacuzzi adjacent to one of the suites. Breakfast on the veranda or in the sunny bay-window parlor usually includes a baked treat. You'll feel quite comfortable here, whether celebrating a special occasion or just looking for a lovely place in which to relax near the sea.

VENICE BEACH HOUSE, No. 15, Thirtieth Avenue, Venice, CA 90291; (213) 823-1966. Vivian and Phil Boesch, owners; Elaine Burke, hostess. A bit of Spanish and French spoken. Nine rooms, several with private bath. Rates: $50 to $125. Includes continental breakfast. Children over ten; no pets; Visa/MasterCard/American Express. Smoking permitted in porch areas.

DIRECTIONS: from L.A. take 405 to Washington Street and make a right heading towards the ocean. Turn right at Speedway and the house is on the right corner. Parking in the rear. Ten minutes from LAX.

CROWN BED & BREAKFAST

A classic example of the Craftsman style

Designed and built single-handedly in 1905 by Louis B. Easton, who lived next door, this house was created in the spirit of the Arts and Crafts movement. It is a strong statement against mass production and conformity and presents a classic example of the Craftsman style of architecture, featuring hand-hewn wooden interiors and hand-forged metalwork. It is dedicated to a pure aesthetic and functional simplicity.

After being restored by the Pasadena Heritage from original drawings, the building was sold to a group including Jetty and Miller Fong, who assumed stewardship of the historic house. Two purposes were served: the society used the money it realized to restore a second building in Pasadena; the Fongs had the foresight to create Pasadena's first bed and breakfast.

Guest rooms are spacious enough to offer seating areas with comfortable chairs, and several of the rooms have couches that make up into a double bed. Rattan furniture reminiscent of the period and special pieces re-created from Louis B. Easton designs comprise most of the furnishings.

Greeted by hostess Jetty Fong, a visitor will find this a comfortable lodging alternative while attending the Rose Bowl, visiting the civic center and Norton Simon Museum, or enjoying the renaissance of Pasadena's restaurants. Niceties at the Crown include a glass of wine upon arrival, chilled fruit and flowers in rooms, and breakfast in bed.

CROWN BED & BREAKFAST INN, 530 S. Marengo Ave., Pasadena, CA 91101; (818) 792-4031; Miller and Jetty Fong, owners. Five rooms, three baths. Rates: $58 to $75. Includes well presented continental breakfast. Well-behaved children over twelve; no pets; smoking in downstairs common areas only; Visa/MasterCard.

DIRECTIONS: from L.A./Pasadena Freeway, exit 11 becomes Arroya Parkway. Make a right onto California St. and a left onto Marengo.

Left, the house's fine cabinetry exemplifies the best of the Arts and Crafts movement at the turn-of-the-century. Above, copies of Stickley furniture flank the clinker-brick fireplace.

Nesting quail in front of the Wood Thrush Cottage.

and guests can lounge outside when they are not indulging in Santa Barbara's seashore or attractive shops. Breakfast is served on a big old country-pine farm table, and the smell of hot cider, apple muffins and persimmon bread fills the house.

BLUE QUAIL INN, 1908 Bath Street, Santa Barbara, CA 93101; (805) 687-2300. Jeanise Suding, hostess. Nine rooms, shared and private baths in main house and four cottages. Rates: $50 to $75 winter; $60 to $85 summer. Children over twelve; no pets; smoking preferred outside; Visa/MasterCard.

DIRECTIONS: US-101 south, exit at Mission Street offramp and turn left. Proceed one block and turn right onto Castello Street. In one block turn left onto Pedregosa Street. Proceed one block and turn left onto Bath Street. US-101 north, take the Arrellaga Street offramp. Proceed two blocks and turn left onto Bath Street.

BLUE QUAIL INN

Guest rooms named after birds

Country charm, piping hot popovers, and picnic lunches to take along on bike rides await guests at Jeanise Suding's Blue Quail Inn. Although Santa Barbara can be stylish and chic, this inn suits those who are looking for straightforward comfort.

The style of this complex, consisting of a main house and four cottages, is very contemporary, and Jeanise has decorated the rooms with big, beautiful country quilts, porcelain farm animals, canopied beds, and overstuffed chairs. A choice of guest rooms includes the Whippoorwill, the Meadowlark, the Wood Thrush, and the Nightingale, as well as five other rooms also named after birds.

There is plenty of yard surrounding the cottages,

Hostess Jeanise Suding and friend Rodney.

THE PARSONAGE

The European tradition

Hilde Michelmore's energy, style, and warmth are evident the moment you step through the door of the Parsonage. This 1892 Queen Anne house is filled with the ebullient personality of its hostess. Raised in Europe, with its tradition of hospitality, Hilde receives guests graciously and makes their visits memorable. All comes effortlessly, whether she is serving a lavish breakfast of French toast or apple pancakes, sharing the afternoon cocktail hour, or helping someone plan an evening.

In the living room, an emerald green and deep purple Oriental carpet serves as a vibrant backdrop for the antiques and original redwood trim that are stylishly combined with modern furnishings.

Upstairs, the Las Flores room, with its unusual marble-topped sideboard and antique armoire, recaptures the era when this building was a rectory.

Mirrored bedroom set in the Honeymoon Suite.

The spacious outdoor deck is made for sun worshipers, and it is easy to curl up in one of the lounge chairs with a good book. Breakfast is often served at one of the umbrella-covered tables, and if light exercise is in order, the famous mission is a short and pleasant walk away.

THE PARSONAGE, 1600 Olive Street, Santa Barbara, CA 93101; (805) 962-9336; Hilde Michelmore, hostess. Fluent in German. Five rooms, each with private bath. Rates: $55 to $105. Includes full, delicious breakfast. Children over fourteen welcome; no pets; smoking allowed. Beautiful pearl-grey cat in residence.

DIRECTIONS: from the south on US-101, exit onto State Street. Follow State and take a right onto Arrellaga Street. Proceed to Olive Street and the house is on the corner. From the north on US-101, exit onto Arrellaga Street and proceed to Olive Street.

Hostess Hilde Michelmore and her Russian blue cat.

The hosts use candles and tremendous bouquets of flowers to create a romantic mood.

THE BAYBERRY INN

New England opulence

"I want my guests to feel as if they are returning to visit a well-to-do grandma," comments Carlton Wagner of Carlton Wagner Designs. He and Keith Pomeroy, who has a background in catering, have combined their talents to provide a gracious in-town bed and breakfast. No detail is too insignificant, no decoration too extravagant for this ambitious showcase restoration. The owners have been successful in achieving an opulence undreamed of by grandma.

Seventeenth-century Italian walnut chairs covered with flamboyant tapestry surround the apricot marble dining table. A grand piano entices those who are musically inclined, and a dozen or so candles on the living room mantel set a luxurious mood. Guest rooms are named and color coordinated for different berries. The Blueberry Room has its own sun room and all rooms have canopied beds.

The transition from the house to the large yard is heralded by the sweet sound of zebra finches chirping on the sun porch. Once outside, classical sculpture, a gazebo, and a recessed Victorian lattice for plantings offer an elegant outdoor retreat.

THE BAYBERRY INN, 111 West Valerio Street, Santa Barbara, CA 93101; (805) 682-3199; Carlton Wagner and Keith Pomeroy, hosts. Seven rooms, all with private bath; five with fireplaces. Rates: $55 to $105. Includes a full breakfast with gourmet egg dish. Children over twelve; no pets; smoking on outside deck; Visa/MasterCard/American Express. Three terriers in residence.
DIRECTIONS: from the south via US-101: after passing the State Street exit, go one block and turn right onto Chapalla. Continue 13 blocks to Valerio Street and the inn is on the left corner. From the north via US-101: at the Mission Street exit, take a left onto Mission Street and a right onto De La Vina. Continue on De La Vina and take a left onto Valerio Street. The Inn is one block on the right.

RED ROSE INN

Delightful Victorian in Santa Barbara

Chosen by the Santa Barbara Historical Society to be featured in *Survivors*, a publication recording the city's finest examples of Victorian architecture, this inn is a delight. There is a crisp, coordinated charm to the place that reflects the fresh and youthful personalities of its hosts, Neile Ifland, who likes to bake, and Rick Ifland, a serious runner. Owners of a tandem bike, they insist it is the only way to see the town or beach, especially with the picnic lunches that Neile loves to pack.

There is something in every corner of the house to evoke a smile: a stained-glass window, a bed with a direct provenance to Abraham Lincoln, and a framed ladies' fan that doubles as an 1897 calendar, with a blond cherub decorating each of the months.

A portrait of a woman hangs in each of the guest rooms, and although they are not famous opera singers or infamous women of the Wild West, they are held in high esteem. This is not surprising for they are Neile and Rick's great grandmothers, whose presence reflects the warm sentiment you find here.

RED ROSE INN, 1416 Castillo, Santa Barbara, CA 93101; (805) 966-1470; Neile and Rick Ifland, hosts. Four rooms, two with private bath. Rates: $55 to $75 double. Well-behaved children during the week are welcome; no pets; smoking outside only; Visa/MasterCard.

DIRECTIONS: from US-101, exit onto Arrellaga Street. Proceed to Castillo Street one block east.

Sunset signals the time for wine and cheese at the Red Rose.

Left, four shades of rose grace the restored building. A multitude of windows illuminate the rooms, as in the one above.

ROSE VICTORIAN INN

Spectacular inside and out

This 1885 landmark home, once surrounded by walnut tree farms, continues to dominate the horizon of the farmlands of San Luis Obispo County. Painted in four shades of rose, it rises toward the sky, a majestic fifty-five-foot four-story Victorian.

The inn has become a romantic mecca. More than one hundred brides have walked along the thirty-foot rose arbor to the gazebo to meet their grooms. Celebrating anniversaries at the Rose Victorian is a tradition many couples still honor.

The appeal of the Rose Victorian goes far beyond its imposing stature, given the warmth and whimsy of the Cox family. Enthusiastic, cheerful, and downright hospitable, this family sees to it that guests are comfortable and enjoy themselves. Champagne contributes to conviviality at breakfast, and accompanies a feast of eggs Benedict, artfully prepared by Shelly, and ham-and-cheese or nut-and-raisin stuffed croissants. For the guest on a modified American plan, dinner is included in the room tariff, and the varied, high-quality menu, courteous service, and lovely dining room reflect the Coxes' credo that dining be a fine experience. It is not surprising that the Rose Victorian offers the best dining in the area.

For guests who like to pass a quiet evening, there is a large parlor perfect for deliberating over a jigsaw puzzle or for playing an especially beautiful 1875 rosewood square grand piano. The nearby Great American Melodrama and Vaudeville show is recommended for those who like to hiss and boo at the villain.

ROSE VICTORIAN INN, 789 Valley Road, Arroyo Grande, CA 93420; (805) 481-5566; Diana and Ross Cox, owners, and daughter Shelly, hostess. Shelly speaks Japanese. Six rooms, one with private bath; remaining five rooms share two baths. Each room decorated in keeping with Victorian period. Rates: $90 to $105 modified American plan with full breakfast and six course dinner for two. Weeknight discounts available. Children over sixteen; no pets; smoking in the restaurant and gardens, but not in the house. Collie, Australian shepherd, and three entertaining cats in residence.

DIRECTIONS: located 200 miles north of L.A. and 250 miles south of San Francisco. Take Arroyo Grande exit from US-101. Turn left at the stop sign onto Fair Oaks, go ¼ mile and turn left onto Valley Road. Proceed ¼ mile to the inn.

HERITAGE INN

A congenial stopover in San Luis Obispo

The Heritage Inn is in the heart of San Luis Obispo at the junction of highways 101 and 1. Although several guest rooms look out over hills and a brook, the central location makes this bed and breakfast less of a getaway spot than a home base for exploring the central coast. The famous Hearst Castle is about an hour's drive away, and beaches for sunbathing and sportfishing are nearby.

In contrast to the white, sandy beaches, colorful wildflowers carpet hiking trails through the surrounding countryside. The city's mission, in downtown San Luis Obispo, functions as an information center, and will provide visitors with a history of the area.

HERITAGE INN, 978 Olive Street, San Luis Obispo, CA 93401; (805) 544-7440; Jim and Zella Harrison, owners; Lou, Sherry, Bev, and Judy, hostesses. Rates: $55 to $60, double. Winter, weekday and commercial rates are available. Nine rooms, one with private bath, eight with sink and sharing several baths. Four have fireplaces. Includes continental breakfast of fresh or baked fruit and freshly baked breads. Children over sixteen preferred; no pets; no smoking; Visa/MasterCard/American Express.

DIRECTIONS: from US-101 north, take the Morro Bay exit and turn right onto Santa Rosa and left onto Olive. From US-101 south, take the Santa Rosa Street exit and proceed straight across Santa Rosa onto Olive Street.

Romantic turn-of-the-century décor.

THE PICKFORD HOUSE

Just ten minutes from Hearst Castle

The Pickford House is a peculiar mixture of eras—a recently built Victorian structure with a flashy black and white tiled entryway that leads to a 125-year-old mahogany back bar from the Buffalo Hilton. Here a caribou head over a vintage silver jukebox vies for your attention with a yellow, turquoise, and pink player piano that glows in the dark. Over a hundred different rolls pound out ragtime and blues, and when the occasional musician appears there is live entertainment.

This bed and breakfast was designed and built to accommodate visitors to Hearst Castle, just ten minutes away. The idea came to owner Daryl Goryman when he appeared here for a weekend and couldn't find a place to stay. Each of the guest rooms is named after Hollywood personalities, such as Norma Talmadge, Douglas Fairbanks, Mary Pickford, Clara Bow, and Harold Lloyd. Pictures of the stars hang over the fireplace in the lively bar, and books about them are left lying about the house. The rooms are furnished with antiques that suit their namesakes, and each has a private bath with claw-foot tub, pull-chain toilet, and pedestal sink. The Coke machine in the upstairs hall does not attempt to re-create the Victorian era.

Breakfast is served in the parlor and *ableskivers*, Swedish pancakes, are most popular, with omelets and quiche the runners up.

THE PICKFORD HOUSE, 2555 MacLeod Ave., Cambria, CA 93428; (805) 927-8619; Daryl Goryman, owner; Lisa Evans, manager. Eight rooms, each with private bath. Rates: $65 to $90 double; winter rates: $55 to $80. Includes breakfast with Swedish pancakes or quiche. Happy hour and hors d'oeuvres from 3 PM to 6 PM. Visa/MasterCard accepted with surcharge. Children over twelve; no pets; smoking in bar or lobby only. Ten minutes from Hearst Castle

DIRECTIONS: from the south on Rte. 1, take the Cambria exit onto Eaton, then take a left onto First St. Proceed and turn left onto Wood St., then left onto MacLeod. From the north take the Burton exit and proceed past the Cambria Lodge to stop sign and make a right turn onto Eaton. In one block make another right onto Wood and then a left onto MacLeod.

Right, an extravaganza of colorful furnishings marks the lobby/bar/breakfast room.

A fine old home built in 1886 by the town's founder.

COUNTRY HOUSE INN

Formerly the end of the line

During the 1880s Templeton was "the end of the line." Passengers continuing south on the Southern Pacific Railroad often had to wait several days for a stagecoach. The founder of Templeton built himself a mansion not far from the roundhouse, where engines were turned for their journey back north and where he could watch the stages arrive and depart. The town flourished with hotels, restaurants, and saloons. Because the railroad line was extended to San Luis Obispo, the boom in Templeton lasted only three short years, but the founder's home, now the Country House Inn, survives as a reminder of yesteryear.

The hostess, Barbara Ford, has written a booklet, "Bed & Breakfast: An Inn Experience, The Answer Book for Inn Travel Questions." As an experienced innkeeper, she is able to anticipate a guest's concerns and needs. At the same time, visitors have an opportunity to stay in this historic home, surrounded by rose gardens and hummingbirds, which perform at the dining room window.

Nick Milovina, the host, was born and raised on a farm near Stanford. Since buying the bed and breakfast two years ago, he's become an avid gardener, planting "everything Burpee has that I can afford to buy." Seventy or eighty rose bushes, a grape arbor, eight oak trees, daffodils, tulips, hyacinths, and a well-tended vegetable garden supply rainbow colors to these spacious grounds. Nick has become so addicted to the delights of having a green thumb that he takes reservations on a wireless telephone among the rose bushes.

COUNTRY HOUSE INN, 91 Main Street, P.O. Box 179, Templeton, CA 93465; (805) 434-1598; Nick Milovina and Barbara Ford, hosts. Six rooms, two with shared bath downstairs, four with shared bath upstairs. Rates: $55 double; $35 single. Includes continental breakfast. No children under fourteen; no pets; no smoking in the house. Two dogs and three cats in residence but are outside pets.

DIRECTIONS: from the south on US-101, exit at Templeton onto Vineyard Ave. In two blocks turn left onto Main Street and the inn is approximately 1½ miles on the right. From the north on US-101, exit at Templeton onto Main Street and the inn is approximately ½ mile on the left.

MONTEREY

THE JABBERWOCK

Enjoy a breakfast of Razzleberries

Named after the mythical character in Lewis Carroll's poem "Jabberwocky," this Jabberwock is a special bed and breakfast where two themes prevail. First, there is humor in everything that hosts Jim and Barbara Allen undertake. From the presentation of a tantalizing series of mysterious hors d'oeuvres at aperitif hour to the surprise breakfast, everything is a curiosity. Anything from Snarkleberry, Razzleberry, or Frabjous may appear on the menu. The guest rooms have names too: Tulgey Wood, Mome Rath, or Brillig.

The second prevailing theme at the Jabberwock is hospitality, a flair for which Barbara developed during thirteen years spent in the hotel industry. Everything is first quality here, from the lace-trimmed sheets to the special down comforters.

Details have been carefully attended to, such as writing first names of guests on a chalkboard, or leaving binoculars on windowsills for a bay view. Jim, a recently retired captain of the Los Angeles Fire Department, has his own style and penchant for fun, and it is well worth asking him for a tour in the British Beardmore taxi.

Once a convent, the Jabberwock makes a large, elegant home. The living room is luxurious, and the wraparound sun porch is especially inviting. Gardens and a waterfall only enhance what Jim and Barbara have created to make your visit to the Monterey Peninsula memorable.

THE JABBERWOCK, 598 Laine Street, Monterey, CA 93940; (408) 372-4777; Jim and Barbara Allen, hosts. Barbara speaks French, Danish, and Spanish. Five rooms, two with private baths. Of the remaining three rooms, two have sinks and share two well-located, spacious bathrooms. Rates: $75 to $125. Includes imaginative, delicious breakfast, a delectable selection of hors d'oeuvres and warm cookies and milk before bed. No children; no pets; no smoking except on the sun porch; no credit cards. Popular English bull terrier in residence. Four blocks above Cannery Row and famous aquarium.

DIRECTIONS: from Rte. 1 take Rte. 68 west for 2½ miles. Turn right onto Prescott and right onto Pine for one block and then turn left onto Hoffman. The Jabberwock is on the corner of Hoffman and Laine.

Special treats await guests at bed-time.

SEVEN GABLES INN

Museum-quality opulence

Filled with an impressive collection of fine art, statuary, ornamental china, and antique furnishings, the House of the Seven Gables is one of the grandest homes on the Monterey Peninsula. The result of thoughtful choices made over many decades, it is filled with pieces acquired by John and Nora Flatley during their extensive travels. Not bought to be coveted as "museum pieces," the extravagant collection is used and enjoyed by family and guests.

Whether you are discovering an eighteenth-century oil painting or marveling at the detailing on a Sèvres vase, the hosts are delighted you noticed. Six family members, who share various aspects of innkeeping, will be happy to tell you an interesting aside about a particular marble statue or piece of ornate furniture. Notice the beautiful sunset if you happen to be in the dining room. The rays bounce off a monumental crystal chandelier and reflect in a floor-to-ceiling pier mirror.

Since they became innkeepers in 1958, the Flatleys have lovingly tended the flower gardens that border their house and the imposing shoreline. Lovers' Point Beach and the sea are just steps away, and the dramatic Monterey coastline can be seen from each of the inn's twelve guest rooms. Cannery Row is a three-minute drive or a short walk along the waterfront, and the famous Seventeen-Mile Drive begins at the front door.

SEVEN GABLES INN, 555 Ocean View Boulevard, Pacific Grove, CA 93950; (403) 372-4341; John and Nora Flatley and family, owners. Susan, Fred, Ed, and Heather are adult family members involved with the various facets of innkeeping. Spanish, French, and Arabic spoken. Seven rooms in the main house plus several separate cottages and a carriage house, all with full bath. Rates: $65 to $95. Includes continental breakfast that often offers scones or, on summer Sundays, strawberry shortcake. Children over twelve; no pets; no smoking; Visa/MasterCard. Homer, the dog, and Al, the cat, in residence.

DIRECTIONS: from Rte. 1 north take Pacific Grove-Del Monte exit. Take Del Monte (which becomes Lighthouse Ave.) through the tunnel and into Pacific Grove. Go right one block to Ocean View Blvd., then left to Fountain Ave. and the inn. From Rte. 1 south take Pacific Grove-Pebble Beach Exit. Once in Pacific Grove take Forest Ave. to Ocean View Blvd., and then right two blocks to Fountain Ave. and the inn.

Left, the house contains a collection of extraordinary antiques.

Owner and host Dr. Joe Megna greets guests in the lobby.

THE CENTRELLA

A million-dollar revival

Touted by journalists at the turn-of-the-century as "the largest, most commodious, and pleasantly located private boarding house in the Grove," the Centrella is now experiencing a revival. The entirely refurbished million dollar interior, replete with wainscoted hallways, stained-glass and be-veled windows, antique furniture, and electrified gas fixtures, has received the Gold Key Award for "excellence in guest room interior."

A large common room with a marble-faced fireplace serves as a gathering place for guests in the evening as well as for buffet breakfasts that include pastries, fruit, and yogurt. Turrets, bay windows, gingerbread, and graceful porches add to the attractiveness of this vintage hotel. In addition to rooms in the main building, there are five separate cottages with fireplaces, refrigerators, and sitting areas.

Located in the heart of Pacific Grove amid old Victorian homes and redwood trees, the Centrella is a block-and-a-half from the ocean and Lovers' Point. It is a three-minute drive from the soon-to-be-completed, eagerly awaited aquarium.

THE CENTRELLA, 612 Central Avenue, P.O. Box 884, Pacific Grove, CA 93950; (408) 372-3372; Joe and Florence Megna, owners. Fluent Italian, Japanese, and a bit of French. Twenty-seven rooms, which includes twenty individual rooms, two honeymoon attic suites, and five separate cottages with fireplaces, refrigerators, and sitting areas. Rates: $50 to $120. Includes continental breakfast of pastries and fresh fruit, yogurt, and bran and a light repast at Social Hour. Children over twelve in main house; any age in separate cottages; smoking permitted in rooms but not in public areas; wheelchair access to rooms on ground floor; Visa/MasterCard/American Express.

DIRECTIONS: Rte. 1 to Pacific Grove exit, which is Rte. 68.

THE SEA VIEW

Sixty years of hospitality

The broad white sand beaches of the Pacific are a stone's throw from the Sea View Inn's front porch. This three-story, wood-shingle, Craftsman bungalow was built in 1910 and has served as an inn for more than sixty years. Decorated with an eclectic mix of period pieces, the overall atmosphere is relaxed and comfortable.

The house sits on one of the quiet byways that crisscross Carmel. These tree-shaded lanes, free of streetlamps and concrete walks, preserve a rustic charm that nurtures gentle spirits.

The inn is close to Point Lobos, the Carmel mission, and the famous Pebble Beach golf course.

THE SEA VIEW, between 11th and 12th on Camino Real, P.O. Box 4138, Carmel, CA 93921; (408) 624-8778; Marshall and Diane Hydorn, owners; Brenda Narvaez, manager. Some French spoken. Eight rooms, six with private baths. Rates: $45 to $62. Includes buffet-style breakfast of cereals, pastries, and non-sweet breads; egg dish on Sundays. No children under twelve; no pets; smoking on outside porch where ashtrays and chairs are provided; Visa/MasterCard. Wise and all-seeing cat in residence.

DIRECTIONS: take Ocean Ave. exit off Rte. 1 and proceed on Ocean. Turn left onto Camino Real and proceed 5½ blocks to inn.

CHÂTEAU VICTORIAN

Colorful Victorian

One block from the newly renovated Santa Cruz boardwalk, Château Victorian offers a pleasing array of accommodations. Several of the seven bedrooms contain working fireplaces, and all have modern private baths, a sitting area, and a tasteful selection of antique furnishings. For sun-worshipers the inn provides a large brick courtyard, and a wooden deck at the front of the house faces the shoreline bustle.

The boardwalk, painted in brilliant rainbow hues, exudes a magnetic and lively carnival air. Amid an atmosphere filled with the aroma of popcorn, hot dogs, and cotton candy, visitors can ride the roller coaster or play games of chance in the penny arcade.

CHÂTEAU VICTORIAN, 118 First Street, Santa Cruz, CA 95060; (408) 458-9458; Franz Benjamin, host. German spoken. Seven rooms, each with private bath. Rates: $55 to $95. Includes buffet breakfast of croissants or bagels, cream cheese, fruit platters, afternoon and evening refreshments. No children; no pets; no smoking; Visa/MasterCard/American Express.

DIRECTIONS: Rte. 17 into Santa Cruz, which becomes Ocean St. Follow to the end and take a right onto San Lorenzo Blvd. Proceed three blocks to first traffic light and take a left onto Riverside St. Cross over bridge and turn right onto Second St., left onto Cliff St., and right onto First St.

Hosts Marshal and Diane Hydorn and their 1910 Bungalow.

Left, the entrance hall to a splendid Victorian parlor. Above, the Orchard Room, aptly named for its view of the surrounding orchards.

APPLE LANE INN

Enchanting Victorian décor

*A life without festivity
is like a road without an Inn.*
—Democratus (450 B.C.)

Once surrounded by sixty acres of apple orchards, this 1876 Victorian farmhouse retains the flavor of its original setting. Approached along a lane lined with apple trees and an old barn, the view opens onto a quiet patio with a grape arbor and lots of wonderful bright flowers.

All the enchantment of Victorian décor is displayed here, from the mahogany furniture and Oriental rugs in the formal parlor to the bedrooms on the second floor. On the third floor, Victorian conventions give way to an airy country style, where colorful stencils decorate floors, walls, and window shades. Dhurrie rugs with pastel accents combine cheerfully with white walls, painted rafters, and a pitched roof.

Small touches add to the pleasing quality of Apple Lane, such as the polished fresh apples tucked beside each guest's pillow. A collection of antique dolls embellishes one room, and in another a high four-poster bed carved with pineapples symbolizes the hospitality so apparent throughout the inn.

There are books everywhere and lots of wonderful art, from black and white photgraphs by Ansel Adams and Carleton Watkins, to Oriental rubbings and contemporary oils. Rare maps are beautifully displayed, revealing the host's scholarly interest in geography.

APPLE LANE INN, 6265 Soquel Drive, Aptos, CA 95003; (408) 475-6868; Barbara Buckmaster and Peter Farqhuar, owners. Four rooms, two with private ½ baths and shared shower. The two rooms that share a bath have their own sinks. Rates: $60 to $75. Inquire about discounts during the week. Includes a full continental breakfast. Children over twelve; no pets; smoking in the parlors only; Visa/MasterCard.

DIRECTIONS: from Rte. 1 north exit at Seacliff Beach and turn right on four-way stop. Take a left onto Soquel Drive. Proceed slightly over a mile, and just past Cabrillo College look carefully on the right for a sign to Apple Lane. From Rte. 1 south turn left onto Park Avenue and right onto Soquel Ave. Look for a sign on the left just before Cabrillo College.

NEW DAVENPORT BED & BREAKFAST INN

Spectacular coastline, special people

Just nine miles north of Santa Cruz, on Highway 1, the tiny community of Davenport resides along a magnificent stretch of California coastline. A good number of the two hundred populating the village are craftspeople (from a boat builder to a knife maker). Foremost among them are Marcia and Bruce McDougal.

After successfully operating the local Big Creek Pottery School, the McDougals opened the New Davenport Cash Store as an outlet for the school's pottery. It later evolved into a center for an outstanding selection of pottery, jewelry, textiles, and folk art from around the world. Shortly thereafter, they opened the New Davenport Restaurant, a casual establishment that offers wholesome, fine home cooking.

The New Davenport Bed and Breakfast is this energetic couple's newest addition to the community. Rooms are contemporary in design, and each is decorated with artwork and crafts. A wraparound porch on the second story of the main building is a wonderful place to relax and enjoy the beauty of the surrounding landscape.

A generous continental breakfast, which includes mouth-watering cinnamon rolls, is served in the small adjacent building, or guests may repair to the restaurant for a more full-bodied meal. Davenport is a great place to watch the gray whales as they migrate along the coast from January to May, or simply to pause from life's hectic pace.

NEW DAVENPORT BED & BREAKFAST INN, 31 Davenport Avenue, Davenport, CA 95017; (408) 425-1818 or 426-4122; Bruce and Marcia McDougal, owners. Twelve rooms; eight in two-story western-style building with a wrap around porch, four in adjacent restored home. All with private baths. Rates: $45 to $75. Includes a generous continental breakfast in the restaurant or on tray brought to the room, or a credit towards full breakfast. Exceptional cinnamon rolls! Complimentary champagne in each room. Children over twelve; no pets; smoking on the porches, sitting rooms, and dining room, but not in the bedrooms; Visa/MasterCard/American Express.

DIRECTIONS: on Rte. 1, halfway between San Francisco and Monterey Bay. Nine miles north of Santa Cruz. Slow down when you get to Davenport and you'll see it!

Left, wind-blown cypress trees retard erosion of the rugged cliffs at Davenport. Above, hosts Marsha and Bruce McDougal.
OVERLEAF: *San Francisco glistening in the sun, seen from Marin County.*

SAN FRANCISCO

THE INN SAN FRANCISCO

The mood of Old World elegance

The mood at the Inn San Francisco is serene and harmonious. In the parlor, light through thickly fringed Victorian lampshades softly illuminates deep, dark green walls, heavy velvet draperies, and stained glass. Candles flicker on the marble mantel, and pretty porcelain adorns ornate tables.

The feeling of Old World elegance is carried to the bedrooms. There guests find old-fashioned lighting fixtures, Oriental rugs, brass beds—and perhaps a tub discreetly concealed behind a fabric screen or large dressing mirror.

Proprietors Joel Daily and Tony Kramedas added dimension to their inn with an artful blend of contemporary conveniences. A second sitting room contains modular couches, a coffee table covered with books and magazines, a television, and a bulletin board that announces events around town. Slippered guests gravitate to this room to curl up with a book or relax in easy conversation. More luxury is available in the plant-filled solarium, where a hot tub beckons, and a spiral staircase leads to a redwood sundeck.

THE INN SAN FRANCISCO, 943 South Van Ness Avenue, San Francisco, CA 94110; (415) 641-0188; Tony Kramedas and Joel Daily, owners; Miriam Wright, manager, and Genevieve Schulte, hostess. A bit of Greek is spoken by Tony. Fifteen rooms, several with private baths, several with refrigerators, all with marble sinks and furnished in a Victorian tradition. Rates: $46 to $106. Includes hearty buffet breakfast with platter of cut tropical fruits, butter pastries, and hardcooked eggs. Children over 14; no pets; smoking allowed except in the parlor during breakfast; Visa/MasterCard/American Express. Limited parking by reservation.
DIRECTIONS: between 20th and 21st Street on Van Ness.

Guests luxuriate in the hot tub, left, and in the lavish parlor, above.

THE MANSION HOTEL

Intentionally outlandish

The proprietor of the Mansion is Robert Pritikin, the same man who brought you *Christ Was An Adman*, America's most irreverent book on advertising. The place is a visual extravaganza, from the crimson pool table, surrounded by the Broadway set from Edward Albee's *Tiny Alice*, to the mural of pie-eating pigs at a picnic. The Mansion's macaw screeches in the background, while a human-sized Miss Piggy watches guests come and go from her chair on the stairway landing. Nightly performances by Pritikin on the saw, accompanied on the piano by Claudia, the resident ghost, and the weekend magic shows in the music room are examples of the zaniness to be encountered.

In addition to all the sophisticated gimmickry, The Mansion has one of the world's most extensive collections of Bufano sculpture and the building itself is quite splendid. Staying at the Mansion can be outrageous fun, and you will remember it vividly long after you've gone. Pritikin has put together a place that is intentionally outlandish.

THE MANSION HOTEL, 2220 Sacramento Street, San Francisco, CA 94115; (415) 929-9444; Robert C. Pritikin, Master of Ceremonies and owner; Denise Mitidieri, manager. Nineteen rooms, each with bath and special décor. Rates: $129 to $200. Includes breakfast of soft-boiled egg and croissant plus a nightly magic show. No pets; Visa/MasterCard/Diners Club/American Express. Gourmet dining room; David Coyle, master chef.

DIRECTIONS: from LAX, Rte. 101 towards Civic Center, exit at Golden Gate Bridge/Franklin Street. Bear left and proceed up Franklin and turn left onto Sacramento.

The 1887 Mansion.

Gypsy-willow furniture was designed expressly for the inn.

THE WILLOWS

A special peacefulness

There is a special peacefulness to be found at the Willows. Each room features handmade California gypsy-willow beds, chairs, chaises, and tables that were designed and made for the inn. Reflecting the essence of true craftsmanship, the furniture is a perfect blending of the functional and the aesthetic. It is refreshing to be seated in and surrounded by this straightforward and honest furniture in one of the world's most sophisticated cities.

Operated continuously as an inn since 1904, the Willows has recently been renovated in a style fashioned after hostelries in the European tradition. Each of the rooms has its own sink, a wicker basket full of toiletries, and a luxurious terrycloth robe for the short walk to the two bathrooms on each floor. Croissants for breakfast, tea in the afternoon, and brandy nightcaps, delivered to each room, are all part of the gracious hospitality of the house.

THE WILLOWS, 710 14th Street, San Francisco, CA 94114; (415) 431-4770; Rachmael ben-Avram and Gerard Lespinette, owners. French, German, and Chinese spoken. Eleven rooms with four shared baths and four shared shower rooms. Rates $52 to $79. Includes continental breakfast, afternoon tea, and other refreshments in the evening. Children over eight; no pets; Visa/ MasterCard/American Express/Diners Club/Carte Blanche. Direct dial private telephone in each room. Free limousine service in the morning during trade shows. Convenient public transportation.

DIRECTIONS: from the south and LAX, take US-101 north and follow signs to Golden Gate Bridge. Take Mission Street/Van Ness Exit onto Duboce St. Continue on Duboce and turn left onto Market St. Pass the Safeway and turn right onto 14th St.

ALAMO SQUARE INN

A grand era revived

Wayne Corn, who was raised in North Carolina, and Klaus May, a native of Germany's Rhineland, make this the pleasant place it is. Innkeeper Wayne's brand of southern hospitality and resident-chef Klaus's European-style breakfasts herald the revival of that elegant era when continental-style accommodations and gracious service were commonplace.

Eliza Baum, a woman of vision, built this mansion. Inspired by the Midwinter Fair of 1894, with its far-reaching effects on building styles, the house is a blend of Queen Anne and Neo-Classical Revival. A grand staircase with hand-carved balusters, a stained-glass skylight, and large parlors hark back to an era when luxurious space was fashionable. Wainscoting, rich oak floors, and elegant furnishings blend with an eclectic collection of treasures from Afghanistan, India, Iran, and China.

A combination of Queen Anne and Neo-Classical Revival.

A contemporary look characterizes the furnishings of the morning room and adjacent solarium. Flower gardens have paths and decks to ensure a leisurely full breakfast or a relaxing time in the sun.

ALAMO SQUARE INN, 719 Scott Street, San Francisco, CA 94117; (415) 922-2055; Wayne Morris Corn, host; Klaus May, resident chef. Five rooms, each with private bath decorated in period pieces with oriental influence. Rates: $75 to $225. Includes hearty breakfast of eggs Benedict, omelets, breads. Special dinners and conferences by arrangement. Children over twelve; no pets; smoking in the solarium only; Visa/MasterCard/American Express.

DIRECTIONS: located on the west side of Alamo Square, ten blocks west of the Civic Center and two blocks north of Fell.

Sumptuous parlors blend Victorian and Oriental appointments.

VICTORIAN INN ON THE PARK

Elegance in a superb location

Directly across from the verdant expanse of Golden Gate Park, the Victorian Inn on the Park was recently awarded landmark status. Innkeepers Lisa and William Benau's splendid Queen Anne-style inn was built in Queen Victoria's diamond jubilee year, 1897, and it supports one of the last remaining belvedere towers in the city. This grand, nine-thousand-square-foot mansion is filled with stunning architectural detail, from spectac-

ular fireplaces and broad staircases to elaborate wainscoting in spacious hallways. The fine inlaid wood floors and oak paneling in the dining room are good examples of the distinctive style of architect William Curlett and the impeccable taste of Congressman Clunie, who lived in the house for thirty years.

With advance notice, Lisa and Bill will present a chilled bottle of champagne to their newly arrived guests; they will make dinner reservations and confirm theater tickets as well. For the business traveler, the library is equipped with a large desk and telephone, and meetings or business luncheons are easily accommodated. Only ten minutes by car from downtown San Francisco, the Victorian Inn on the Park offers convenience as well as elegance.

VICTORIAN INN ON THE PARK, 301 Lyon Street, San Francisco, CA 94117; (415) 931-1830; Lisa and William Benau, hosts. Six rooms, each with private bath. Rates: $75 to $105. Includes continental breakfast of fresh fruits, freshly baked breads, and croissants. Children under ten discouraged; no pets; smoking is allowed with consideration to the preferences of other guests; Visa/MasterCard/American Express.

DIRECTIONS: from the airport, take US-101 and follow signs to Golden Gate Bridge. Exit at Fell Street and proceed on Fell approx 9/10ths of a mile to Lyon and the inn. From the south on US-101, exit at Lombard Street. Turn right onto Divisadero and proceed approx three miles. Take a right onto Fell and in three blocks a right onto Lyon.

Left and above, attention to detail distinguishes this lavish Victorian.

ARCHBISHOP'S MANSION

Where bed and breakfast achieves eminence

Quite simply, this is the most spectacular place to stay in San Francisco. Built for the archbishop of San Francisco in 1904, it survives today for the pleasure of its guests. The original three-story open staircase, with carved mahogany columns, soars upward to a sixteen-foot stained-glass dome. The expansive entry, hallways, and large rooms are characteristic of the Second French Empire style and suggest a grand country manor. Magnificently carved mantelpieces adorn eighteen fireplaces throughout the house, and high arched windows reflect the grandeur of its era.

Whatever has frayed with the passage of time has been restored with integrity. The resplendent painted ceiling in the parlor is fashioned after the decorative detail of a nineteenth-century Aubusson carpet. A stunning environment is created by the blending of Belle Epoque furnishings with Victorian and Louis XIV statuary, paintings, and bronze chandeliers.

Because Davis Symphony Hall and the opera house are nearby, limousine service for special evenings is provided. This kind of service is typical of the professional and accommodating style of proprietors Jonathan Shannon and Jeffrey Ross, who perfected the art of hospitality while presiding over the highly respected Spreckles Mansion. Anyone spending time at the Archbishop's Mansion is certain to feel pampered by the personal attention of a singular staff amid such resounding elegance.

THE ARCHBISHOP'S MANSION, 1000 Fulton Street, San Francisco, CA 94117; (415) 563-7872; Jonathan Shannon and Jeffrey Ross, owners. Fifteen rooms, all with private baths. Ten rooms have fireplaces, several are full suites with sitting rooms. Extraordinary décor. Rates: $88 to $300. Includes elaborate breakfast. Children discouraged; no pets; smoking is restricted to private rooms and Smoking Room; Visa/MasterCard/American Express. Off-street parking for eight cars and easy street parking. There is a restaurant for guests; the public rooms are available to guests for cocktail parties and conferences; catering service.

DIRECTIONS: on northeast corner of Alamo Square at Steiner and Fulton. Alamo Square is six blocks west of the Civic Center and one block north of Fell.

Left, a sculptured headboard, from a French castle. Above, the mansion seen from Alamo Square Park.

FAY MANSION INN

A majestic survivor of the earthquake

It is common belief that San Francisco's first operas were performed in the music room here by Maude Fay, a celebrated singer. Her family occupied this house from 1874 until 1957, and Maude counted Enrico Caruso as one of her many notable houseguests.

Understated elegance is the keynote here. One of the two tastefully appointed parlors serves as the music room, where a glistening black Kawai piano appears like a piece of sculpture. In the main parlor is one of the city's three hand-painted and stenciled ceiling frescoes still intact from pre-Earthquake days. Its delicacy is breathtaking, and its preservation is a blessing. Also surviving are the original brass and pot-metal chandeliers, with gaslight fixtures and globes beneath matching rosettes.

Standing majestically in the main parlor is a signed rosewood bibliothèque carved in the 1870s, and an 1860s trumeau appears in its original unpainted state. In each of the bedrooms there are charming accents. A beaded handbag and knitted shawl lie across the foot of the bed in the Celebration Suite, and an antique lace dress hangs on the back of the door. Opera masks and elbow-length kid gloves adorn the Maude Fay Room, and there is plum wine with fortune cookies in the Madame Butterfly Room. Godiva chocolates tucked in a music box and a selection of French perfumes are just two of the touches indicative of the pleasantries here.

This intimate, romantic home can become a backdrop for a formal recital or a catered sit-down dinner, and both Sherris Goodwin, the owner, and Sandra Powell, the manager, are gracious and professional. The level of sophistication here is on a par with the best bed and breakfasts in San Francisco.

FAY MANSION INN, 834 Grove Street, San Francisco, CA 94117; (415) 921-1816; Sherris Goodwin, owner; Sandra Powell, general manager. Working knowledge of Spanish, German, and French. Five rooms, with two shared baths upstairs and ½ bath on main floor. Rates $58 to $125. Includes elaborate continental breakfast with a variety of cheeses, fruits, muffins, and unusual strudels and pastries. Confer with the manager regarding children under twelve; no pets; smoking permitted only on the porches and in the garden; Visa/MasterCard/American Express.

DIRECTIONS: on Grove Street, two blocks south of Alamo Square. Alamo Square is six blocks west of the Civic Center.

Left, original gas fixtures and painted ceiling in the exquisite parlor. Above, the Celebration Suite, enhanced by a marble fireplace, a mirrored 1870s walnut armoire, and a Louis XIV desk.

INN ON CASTRO

Contemporary exuberance

In a town of traditionally furnished Victorian bed and breakfasts, the interior of this inn is very contemporary. Bedrooms, individually styled, are visually exciting—one includes a collection of hand-painted birds and another Oriental paper umbrellas.

Besides his penchant for interior design, innkeeper Joel Roman is also an artist. His bright, exuberant paintings of plant forms and glass objects hang throughout the house and underscore the playfulness of the decorating scheme.

Reflected on a chrome coffee table are dozens of pieces of blue glassware, while hundreds of brass, papier-mâché, stone, wood, and other ornaments cover the sideboard in the dining room. Lovingly collected are countless china place settings and interesting flatware. It is possible to spend a year here and never breakfast with the same tableware.

A radiant glass collection.

Joel is the quintessential innkeeper. If there is anything that can be provided for or arranged, consider it done. Whether you ask or not, you are likely to have nice things happen on your behalf.

INN ON CASTRO, 321 Castro Street, San Francisco, CA 94114; (415) 861-0321; Joel M. Roman, owner. French, Spanish, and fluent Italian. Five rooms with 2½ baths, shared. Rates $60 to $75. Includes continental breakfast of which half the fun is the table setting. Children "one at a time and well-behaved;" no pets; smoking permitted in bedrooms, but not in upstairs living or dining rooms; Visa/MasterCard/American Express. Bart subway and other public transportation at the doorstep. Restaurants within walking distance.

DIRECTIONS: located on Castro Street, just north of the intersection where Market, Castro, and 17th Streets meet.

The décor includes paintings by the host.

BERKELEY

An exceptional view of the bay

With an exceptional view of San Francisco Bay, this house is poised on top of one of Berkeley's highest hills. It is a rambling Mediterranean-style villa—spacious, unaffected, and inviting. Soon after you arrive, you'll feel as if this could be home.

The library, fine works of art, and seventeenth-century antiques reflect the broad interests of the hostess, a freelance editor and interviewer.

Several small gardens surround the house, devoted to elaborate plantings of cacti and succulents, ferns, roses, fruit trees, and crimson bougainvillea. Hummingbirds hover over all. The hostess is exuberant about sharing the gardens as well as her knowledge of the area.

BED & BREAKFAST, Berkeley, CA; Rosemary Levenson, hostess. French, Italian, and some German. Three rooms, one with king-size bed and private bath, two with twin beds and shared bath; all with wonderful views. Rates: Moderate, Including lovely breakfast. Children welcome; no pets; television, telephones, and limited use of kitchen. Domestic animals include a dog and a cat. *Represented by Bed & Breakfast International.*

Rosemary Levenson with her beloved golden retriever.

GOLDEN GATE PARK

Featured in *Sunset* magazine

It is easy to see why this house was featured in *Sunset*; an appreciation for the arts is obvious as one enters.

This three-story turn-of-the-century home has much to catch the eye: a brightly colored floor-to-ceiling tapestry, an unusual contemporary painting, a blueprint of a Denver and Rio Grande steam locomotive. Examples of folk art line the kitchen walls, with memorabilia and unusual utensils creating a mosaic effect.

Golden Gate Park, the De Young Museum, and the Japanese Tea Garden are all within walking distance. Clement Street, which features many of San Francisco's finest restaurants, is just around the corner.

BED & BREAKFAST, Golden Gate Park area, San Francisco, CA. Three rooms, one with sitting room furnished with antiques, private bath, 6'7" double bed, television, and telephone. Two modern rooms on third floor with shared bath and shower, double bed, television, stereo, sitting area, and telephone connection. Rooms are very sunny and large with good desk and work space. Rates: moderate, including hearty continental breakfast. Dog in residence. *Represented by Bed & Breakfast International.*

GOLD COUNTRY

Folk art and fine folk

Only after talking to the Hanford House's proprietors, Ron Van Anda and Sandra Whitson, does one find out that this classic building only looks and feels as though it were a hundred years old. Located in Sutter Creek, it is a two-story brick storefront that houses an antiques shop and an adjacent inn. Ron gave a great deal of thought to the western-style storefront he wanted to build. His respect for the past, a strong sense of history, and his natural good taste resulted in a building that adds to the character of the well-preserved town of Sutter Creek.

The mere presence of the Hanford House further enhances Sutter Creek's reputation as the antiques capital of the gold country. Ron and Sandra's private collection of folk art is singularly outstanding, and their shop is filled with an exciting array of things selected from coast to coast. Everything from a $35 birdcage to a $3,500 trade sign for a livery stable can be discovered here.

In the guest rooms there is a comfortable blending of country pine armoires, pine tables, and antiques with contemporary couches and armchairs. A prairie landscape, a hand-painted Chinese chest, a photographic portrait of an Indian chief, or a Remington print may decorate your room. In addition to the visual delights here, the hospitality is first class.

THE HANFORD HOUSE, Highway 49, 3 Hanford Street, P.O. Box 847, Sutter Creek, CA 95685; (209) 267-0747; Ron Van Anda, Sandra Whitson, hosts. Nine rooms, each with modern bath and ceiling fans. Rooms are newly constructed with high ceilings, are exceptionally large and beautifully appointed. Honeymoon suite has a fireplace. Rates: $45 to $100; weekdays 10% less. Includes hearty breakfast of pastries, muffins, and platter of fruits & cheeses. Complimentary wine in each room. No children under twelve; no pets; non-smokers rooms available; Visa/MasterCard. Facilities for handicapped include ramp and room custom-built to accommodate a wheelchair.

DIRECTIONS: located on Highway 49 near Main Street. The only two-story brick building in town!

Left, the sitting room. Above, hosts Ron Van Anda and Sandra Whitson surrounded by their unique collection of folk art.

BOTTO COUNTRY INN

Across from the old Eureka mine

The Botto Country Inn sits directly across from what was the most productive vein of gold in the Mother Lode, the Eureka Mine. Hosts Stan and Mary Ann Stanton believe their two-story frame farmhouse gives visitors a true feeling for this historic area. From the broad and expansive porch, guests can see the stone granary that was once a thriving saloon. The age-worn structure conjures up visions of the miners who came to the saloon to celebrate a strike or to blot out their losses in a mighty oblivion.

The inn is built on a hill overlooking the town of Sutter Creek, one of the prettiest and best-preserved villages in the entire gold country.

BOTTO COUNTRY INN, 11 Sutter Hill Road, Sutter Creek, CA 95685; (209) 267-5519; Stan and Mary Ann Stanton, owners. Five bedrooms with two shared baths. Rates: $53.50. Winter rates. Includes full breakfast of potatoes, scrambled eggs, sautéed vegetables, smoked ham in orange sauce or fritatas and sausage, french rolls, popovers. No credit cards. Exceptional pets and well-behaved children over ten welcomed. No smoking in bedrooms or bathrooms. Two cats, three ducks, and a goose named Lucy in residence.

DIRECTIONS: from north on Rte. 49 go through Sutter Creek up hill and turn left onto Sutter Hill Road. Proceed and you will see a stone building and Botto House on your right. From the south on Rte. 49 as you come down a hill before the town of Sutter Creek take a right onto Sutter Hill Road.

1871 stone granary adjacent to the 1914 farmhouse.

DUNBAR HOUSE

History and homey comfort

Dunbar House emanates romance, homey comfort, and history in equal measure. Innkeepers John and Barbara Carr are dedicated to the pursuit of serving their guests, and they succeed beautifully. A professional nurse for twenty years, Barbara provides a warm, relaxed atmosphere in which visitors can unwind. As she explains, "Guests come here to get away from it all, to enjoy the peace and quiet of the setting, and to regenerate the spirit. We constantly learn from them and love the variety of people who come to stay with us."

The town of Murphys is refreshingly simple. Main Street is filled with an attractive group of specialty shops, a museum, an old-fashioned ice cream parlor, and a small selection of restaurants. An abundance of well-preserved buildings evoke the days when Murphys was "Queen of the Sierras." Local lore has it that in just two weeks during the year 1860, miners took an unprecedented $90,000 worth of gold from nearby mines.

DUNBAR HOUSE 1880, P.O. Box 1375, 271 Jones Street, Murphys, CA 95247; (209) 728-2897; John and Barbara Carr, hosts. Portugese spoken. Five rooms, two shared baths. Rates: $45 to $55. Mid-Winter, mid-week discounts. Includes buffet continental breakfast with assorted cheese board, a variety of cereals and breads, and fresh fruit in season. Children over ten; no pets; smoking on the porches or in garden; no credit cards. Nearby is the Calaveras Big Tree State Park and several caverns and caves worth exploring.

DIRECTIONS: from Rte. 49 proceed to Angel's Camp. Go east on Rte. 4 for nine miles to the Business District turnoff. Take a left at the stop sign and the house is on the left at the Historical Monument.

Hostess Jane Grover likes to surprise guests with her period clothes.

OAK HILL RANCH

Keeping Victorian traditions alive

The opening scenes of *Little House on the Prairie* were shot within a mile of this yellow ranch house. No TV fictions here: the rolling hills, grazing cattle, and good clean air are a way of life in this part of the country.

The ranch reflects the tireless determination of its hosts, Sanford and Jane Grover, who twenty-five years ago began collecting Victorian turn posts, balconies, railings, mantelpieces, doorways, and other turn-of-the-century relics that could be salvaged and incorporated into their recently built home. The result—a replica of a turn-of-the-century ranch house that is open, spacious, and airy.

Devoted to Victorian traditions, Sanford remains active in the Horseless Carriage Club of America, of which he was president and board member for thirteen years, and Jane, on occasion, loves to dress in period clothing. They always have at least one antique car. Both are active in community affairs, especially at the regional museum, which preserves the mining, logging, and railroad histories of the area.

Surrounded by fifty-odd acres at the end of a long country lane, Oak Hill Ranch is everyone's ideal western farmhouse.

OAK HILL RANCH, 18550 Connally Lane, P.O. Box 307, Tuolumne, CA 95379; (209) 928-4717. Sanford and Jane Grover, hosts. Three bedrooms with two shared baths in main house, plus a separate cottage with kitchen, living room, and fireplace ideal for honeymooners or families. Rates: $40 to $68. Includes a full country breakfast that is a delightful event. Children over fourteen; no pets; smoking on the outside porches and decks only; no credit cards.

DIRECTIONS: from Rte. 108, take Tuolumne Rd. to Carter St. Follow Carter St. south to the schoolyard and turn left onto Elm St. Take a right onto Madrone St. which turns into Apple Colony Rd. The sign for Oak Hill is on the left and will point you to Connally Lane. Proceed to the end of the lane.

A dramatic Victorian home, beautifully restored.

COMBELLACK-BLAIR HOUSE

A leap back in time

Walking into a bedroom at Combellack-Blair, one leaps back in time. It is as though the original owner of the house had just stepped away and left an assortment of combs, a hand mirror, and an enameled powder dish on her vanity. The pincushion is studded with needles and pins, and the embroidery, only partially finished, is set aside. Light glowing from the deeply fringed lampshade casts a soft pink shadow on the rocking chair, and the candles atop the washstand appear to be recently snuffed.

Oriental rugs and a collection of period furnishings in the front parlor recall the 1890s, when the prominent clothier, William Hill Combellack built this home. Leading to the second floor and upward to the tower is an elegant spiral staircase.

Cecile and Jim Mazzuchi purchased the Combellack home after the family had lived there for seventy-nine years. Because the house is so beautiful and so much a part of Mother Lode history, the Mazzuchis decided to provide lodgings so that they could share it with others.

COMBELLACK-BLAIR HOUSE, 3059 Cedar Ravine, Placerville, CA 95667; (916) 622-3764; Cecile and Jim Mazzuchi, hosts. Two rooms with a shared bath. Victorian décor. Rates: $55. Includes a full breakfast with such things as home-made country sausage or sourdough pancakes, baked eggs, homemade English muffins, and in the afternoons, various cakes and three kinds of freshly baked cookies. No children; no pets; smoking allowed on outside balcony or porches; no credit cards. Snoopy is the dog in residence. Placerville is in the foothills of the Sierra Nevada mountains with many historic sites nearby.

DIRECTIONS: from Sacramento on Rte. 50, exit onto Bedford and then make a right onto Main St. At the monument, take a right onto Cedar Ravine and the house is on the left.

MURPHY'S INN

A third-generation innkeeper

"A good innkeeper provides his guests with as many comforts as possible, whether it's keeping a fire blazing on the hearth or helping to plan a day of sightseeing."

A heritage of innkeeping that spans seventy-five years has imbued Marc and Rose Murphy with a true understanding of the nature of the business. Murphy's Inn was built in 1866 as an estate for a famous gold baron. One of the loveliest homes in town, it is also among the most pleasant inns in all the Mother Lode country. The living room is filled with lovely antiques, and the lace curtains and floral wallpapers in the bedrooms gently evoke the past.

From the big and sunny breakfast room, guests watch Marc, in the open kitchen, as he concocts a delicious morning repast that might include Belgian waffles or coddled eggs. Each bedroom has a call button, which will bring Marc or Rose to the door bearing a breakfast tray.

A sports enthusiast, Marc loves to share his knowledge of the area. Visitors enjoy excellent cross-country and downhill skiing, swimming, jogging, and golf privileges at the nearby Auburn Country Club.

MURPHY'S INN, 318 Neal Street, Grass Valley, CA 95945; (916) 237-6873; Marc and Rose Murphy, hosts. Seven rooms, five with private bath. Rates: $48 to $68. Includes full breakfast with coddled eggs or Belgian waffles. Mid-week discounts, business rates, ski packages. Well-behaved children; nearby kennel facilities for pets; smoking permitted; major credit cards. Parakeets, Jerry the cat, and Pearl the Staffordshire bull terrier in residence.

DIRECTIONS: from the south, take Rte. 49 north to Grass Valley and exit at Marysville-Colfax. Turn left at the first stop sign onto south Auburn and then left at second stoplight which is Colfax Ave. Continue three blocks to the corner of Neal and School Street.

The gracious interior suggests a genteel lifestyle.

BEAR RIVER MT. FARM

Down-home country feeling

If you're looking for a spot off the beaten track, where you can have a small cottage to yourself, then Bear River Mountain Farm is the haven you're after. Quiet and secluded, the farm has a down-home country feeling. You can sit by the fireplace all night, and at dawn you can do a little fishing in the creek just outside the door.

Also outside the door are the resident cows, Samantha, Elizabeth, and Ellen. There are also plenty of chickens, lots of bullfrogs, an occasional great gray heron, and the donkey farm across the road. Other activities that can be pursued nearby are tubing down the Bear River, panning for gold, or driving to the lakes for a picnic and some serious fishing.

The whole house must be rented, and it is ideal for a family with children and pets, or for the young at heart. Bear River Mountain Farm provides the opportunity to discover the pleasures of being in your own little barnyard.

BEAR RIVER MT. FARM, 21725 Placer Hills Road, Colfax, CA 95713; (916) 878-8341; Lynne Lewis, hostess. Three rooms accommodating six people in a totally separate two-story cottage. One bath with tub and shower. Rates: $45.00; $12.50 for each additional adult and $7.50 for each additional child under 16. Weekly rates available. Includes simple continental breakfast and an evening's worth of firewood. Fresh eggs can be collected and cooked as you wish. Children welcome; pets are fine (boarding fee if you bring a horse); smoking permitted; no credit cards.

DIRECTIONS: on Rte. 80 North, exit at Placer Hills turnoff. Proceed over freeway and turn left onto Placer Hills Road. Proceed under railroad trestle, and continue on Placer Hills for two miles. The no. is on a mailbox on the left and the house is on the right.

A rustic farmhouse with real chickens.

No-nonsense lions guard the entrance.

THE VICTORIAN

A museum of antiques, silver, and crystal

After a career in retail clothing and a stint as the first woman president of Auburn's chamber of commerce, Maurine Cook is now raising funds to restore Auburn's capitol building. Having traveled the world over, she has ensconced herself atop a hill in a 134-year-old house centered on seven acres overlooking the town of Auburn. With interests as far reaching as the 4-H club and the D.A.R., Maurine is as tenacious as they come, and there is little she is not up to handling with authority and style.

The Victorian, one of the oldest homes in the area, is a museum of antiques, silver, and crystal collected over a lifetime. It has a formal living room and an elegant dining room. For relaxing, the pool, the hot tub, and the well-tended gardens are especially inviting.

Maurine is protective of her privacy, so it is especially important to call ahead. Once she expects you, however, she will show you how much she loves to provide a home for travelers, and obviously succeeds. "Hardly a guest leaves here without throwing their arms around me and giving me a big hug," she grins.

THE VICTORIAN, P.O. Box 9097, Auburn, CA 95603; (916) 885-5879; Maurine Cook, owner. Three rooms with 1½ shared baths. Rates: $45 to $55. Includes full breakfast of waffles (made from grandma's recipes), fruits, bacon or ham. Children over twelve; no pets; smoking is permitted, but not in the bedrooms; no credit cards. Pool, hot tub and garden, patio and gazebo.

DIRECTIONS: call for directions; the home is open by appointment only.

WINE COUNTRY

THISTLE DEW INN

Featuring Gustav Stickley

Because it houses a fine collection of Gustav Stickley furniture, the Thistle Dew Inn is of particular interest. The aesthetic precursor to Frank Lloyd Wright, Stickley's Mission Revival furniture, *circa* 1900, is becoming increasingly popular. As Stickley later stated, "I merely tried to do away with needless ornamentation and return to the plain principles of construction . . . to make furniture that would be durable, comfortable, and fitted to the place it was to occupy and the work it had to do."

Here, the collection is handsomely incorporated throughout the inn, from the porch swing to the dining room table and living room furniture. The result is a quiet, understated elegance, further enhanced by Lisa LaBoskey, the warm and attentive hostess.

Perfectly located, the Thistle Dew Inn is just three doors away from Sonoma's beautiful and historic plaza, which houses part of the Mission San Francisco de Solano. Two cheese factories, a sausage factory, a chocolate store, several bakeries, galleries, restaurants, and an interesting collection of shops and boutiques surround the plaza, which is perfect for a picnic lunch of local cheese, bread, and Sonoma wine. After exploring the plaza, all the wineries of the Sonoma Valley await you.

THISTLE DEW INN, 171 West Spain Street, P.O. Box 1326, Sonoma, CA 95476; (707) 938-2909; Lisa LaBoskey, manager. Six rooms, two with private baths, remaining four rooms share two baths. Rates: $60 to $85. Winter rates slightly less. Country cottage at separate location with kitchen, fireplace, enclosed patios, sitting area, and bath plus indoor and outdoor showers. Rates: $100 per night, $450 per week. Includes continental breakfast of a selection of local cheeses and freshly baked goods. Children not encouraged; no pets; no smoking in the rooms; major credit cards. Pillsbury is the cat in residence.

DIRECTIONS: from San Francisco on US-101 turn east onto Rte. 37, then north onto Rte. 121 which adjoins Rte. 12. Follow into Sonoma to plaza and turn left onto Napa Street and then take the next right onto 1st Street West. Take the next left onto West Spain and the inn is the third house on the left.

A Mission-style swing on the front porch with Hostess Lisa LaBoskey.

LA RÉSIDENCE

For lovers of haute cuisine

Gothic Revival built by a New Orleans river pilot.

"I have such wonderful memories of sitting in English country inns with a room full of strangers and everyone trading stories over a glass of wine," mused hostess Barbara Littenberg, "so I thought it would be fun to open my own." Apparently the fun has not faded. Her favorite part of the business is still welcoming guests and sharing experiences over a glass of wine.

Innkeeping suits her so well, in fact, that she has doubled the initial size of La Résidence to include what is affectionately referred to as "the Barn"—a structure decorated in a French country style, with double French doors that open out onto decks and patios. The Main House, an 1870s Gothic Revival, has a distinct southern flavor accented by interesting period antiques.

There are four top restaurants within twenty minutes of the inn: Auberge Soleil, Miramonte, Domain Chandon, and the French Laundry. Haute cuisine is so popular in the area that Barbara plans to conduct cooking seminars with guest chefs in the Barn's professional kitchens. Special wine courses, wine tastings, and tours are offered here.

LA RÉSIDENCE, 4066 St. Helena Highway N., Napa, CA 94558; (707) 253-0337; Barbara Littenberg, hostess. Fifteen rooms total. Main House: seven rooms, four with sitting rooms and private baths, three with fireplaces. Remaining three rooms share two baths. The Barn: eight rooms with sitting area, fireplaces, private baths, balconies or patios. Rates: $60 to $120. Includes expanded continental breakfast including nutbreads and muffins. Children over fourteen; no pets; Visa/MasterCard/American Express.

DIRECTIONS: from San Francisco, US-101 to Rte. 37 to Rte. 12. Proceed onto Rte. 29 to North Napa and turn right just before Bon Apetit restaurant.

A spacious and alluring bedroom adds to the romance of a weekend of wine tasting.

The beautiful Blue Room has a seven-foot carved headboard, and a working Victrola.

GALLERY OSGOOD

Napa Valley's most lavish breakfast

For innkeepers and artists Joan Osgood and Howard Moehrke, the "good life" means delicious food, interesting conversation, the comforts of a lovely home, and art. Joan's special creations include delicate silkscreen prints, on view throughout the house, and a lavish breakfast that ranks among the best in the Napa Valley. Howard, also an expert in computer software, is responsible for the stained-glass that glows from many windows. These colorful, contemporary works of art provide a charming counterpoint to this Queen Anne–style, redwood home, built in 1898. The two guest bedrooms are in keeping with the age of the house—an antique mahogany headboard and hand-crank Victrola add an old-fashioned flavor to the Blue Room, and the Rose Room is filled with wicker and lace. Joan sees to it that guest rooms are scented with fresh flowers, and bouquets often include fragrant blossoms from the inn's camellia trees.

Joan and Howard are able guides to the area

and can summarize the individual attributes of each of the neighboring wineries. These innkeepers are genuinely enthusiastic about life, and they love to share their home and the valley with their guests.

GALLERY OSGOOD, 2230 First Street, Napa, CA 94559; (707) 224-0100; Joan Osgood & Howard Moehrke, hosts. Two rooms, one shared bath. Rates $65 double. Includes lavish, gourmet breakfast of plentiful proportions and guests are invited to join the hosts for a glass of wine. Children over fourteen; no pets; Visa/MasterCard. Pet dog, Heidi is a Llasa Apso and outdoor cat Hershey is part Persian.

DIRECTIONS: from the south on Rte. 29 exit at First Street/ Central Napa. Proceed on exit ramp and take a left onto Second St. In one block take a left onto Seymour St. and then a left onto First St. The inn is on the right.

The living room and adjacent solarium adapt easily for entertaining.

VILLA ST. HELENA

Rooms with vineyard views

Known for successfully integrating buildings with natural environments, architect Robert M. Carrere has succeeded admirably with Villa St. Helena. Constructed as an octagon, with a hillside completing one of its sides, this Mediterranean estate is situated atop twenty glorious acres of oak, bay, and madrona trees. Each suite opens onto the courtyard, and there is a view of the Napa Valley vineyards rolling on for miles beneath your gaze, bringing the countryside indoors.

Hundreds of cymbidium orchids flourish in the courtyard, on the verandas, and in the solarium, all under the watchful eye of owners Ralph and Carol Cotton. Sharing their villa is a joy, and Carol Resnick, the villa's manager, is the consummate innkeeper. Jogging across the courtyard from one suite to another (which says something about the size of the villa as well as her energy), she will cajole you into eating a third helping at breakfast and see to it that you're having a wonderful time.

VILLA ST. HELENA, 2727 Sulphur Springs Avenue, St. Helena, CA 94574; (707) 963-2514; Ralph & Carol Cotton, owners; Carol Resnick, manager. Four Suites, each with private bath and spacious quarters. Rates: $65 to $150. Mid-winter and mid-week rates. Includes a bountiful and delicious breakfast, with a selection of cheeses and bread and a variety of baked or fresh fruits. Guests are invited to join their host and hostesses for wine in the evening. No children; no pets; Visa/MasterCard/American Express. Nutmeg is the cat in residence.

DIRECTIONS: from Rte. 29 take a left onto Sulphur Springs Ave. Proceed approximately 1½ miles and look for sign on mail boxes on the left. Take a left and follow the private driveway ¾ of a mile to the top of the hill.

AMBROSE BIERCE HOUSE

The former home of a literary legend

Set back off the main artery to all the Napa Valley vineyards, this house was home to writer Ambrose Bierce, who mysteriously disappeared in 1913, on a trip to war-torn Mexico. Recalling Bierce's days here, proprietor Kim Thomas has named the suites after figures who touched the writer's life: Lillie Langtry, star of the Edwardian stage; Eadweard Muybridge, father of the motion picture, and Lillie Coit, the legendary belle of San Francisco and Bierce's good friend.

Recently renovated, this charming post-Victorian house has comfortable furnishings and a nicely appointed period look. Beautiful and unusual flowers appear everywhere, all arranged by Kim Thomas, who carries out the smallest details to perfection. Nothing escapes his eye, and no wonder. For eight years, as a scout for an executive-search firm, he traveled and stayed at innumerable hotels. From these experiences he has extracted all of the best innkeeping secrets and brought them home.

Two hundred hours of his research have gone into bedside booklets detailing everything you might want to know about the Napa Valley, including winery information, bicycle and jogging paths, restaurants listed by cuisine, dry cleaning services, and limousines. Whether you are interested in a "country inn massage" or renting a bicycle to tour any of a dozen vineyards, Kim Thomas can arrange it.

THE AMBROSE BIERCE HOUSE, 1515 Main Street, St. Helena, CA 94574; (707) 963-3003; Kim Thomas, owner. Four rooms, two with private baths and two with connecting bath. Designer coordinated décor. Rates: $70 to $80. Includes continental breakfast with fruit course and different types of croissant. Complimentary bottle of wine with the house label. Children twelve and over; no pets; smoking in common areas only, not in the bedrooms; American Express.

DIRECTIONS: fifteen miles north of Napa on Rte. 29, which becomes Main St. On the north end of St. Helena, two doors off Pine St. on the west side of the street.

Memorabilia, from period cameras to vintage firearms, add historical character to the Eadweard Muybridge Room.

There are graceful porches on four sides of the perfectly symmetrical house.

THE INK HOUSE

An architectural achievement

This Victorian farmhouse is an architectural achievement in perfect symmetry. Each side is identical and each looks out on a vineyard. Built a century ago, this intriguing home reflects the character and ingenuity of Theron H. Ink, a man of many interests.

Twelve-foot-high ceilings make the rooms feel large and spacious. The bedrooms have American and English oak and walnut furniture, lace curtains, and handmade quilts. An informal but inviting parlor is furnished with a plum velvet settee and matching side chairs, Victorian marble tables, and an Oriental carpet. Breakfast is served on a large oak table in the crystal-chandeliered dining room. Bran muffins, raisin-carrot or banana-nut cakes, and fresh fruit are offered.

The Clarks moved into the Ink House with their five children in 1967. Ten years later they started their inn. The children still stop by to help with the chores, answer the phone, make reservations, and take over the innkeeping when mom and dad take time off. This is a family-run business that makes other families feel right at home. A glass of sherry from one of the local wineries awaits you.

THE INK HOUSE, 1575 St. Helena Highway, St. Helena, CA 94574; (707) 963-3890; Lois Clark, hostess. Four rooms, each with private bathroom and shower. Furnished with antiques. Rates: $70 to $80. Winter Rates. Includes breakfast of fresh breads and cereals. No children under twelve; no pets; no smoking; no credit cards. Two dogs and two cats in residence but not in guest areas.

DIRECTIONS: at the southwest corner of Rte. 29 and Whitehall Lane, two miles south of St. Helena.

Left, the gigantic, sun-filled bedrooms contain some of their original furnishings.

MADRONA MANOR

A gourmet's bed and breakfast

Built as a vacation retreat for a wealthy San Francisco businessman in 1881, expense appears to have been of no concern here. The ceilings are high, and the several parlors off the hallway are large and elegant. A broad staircase leads to four spacious master suites, each of which either has a large bay window or opens out onto a balcony.

Many of the furnishings in both the Manor and adjacent Carriage House are original to the estate and are important examples of American Victorian Renaissance style. There is an elegant mahogany

four-poster bed dating from the mid-1800s and a full suite of matching carved walnut and burled wood dressers and headboard. The music room of the Manor remains the same, with the original rosewood square grand piano still in place.

What was at one time the billiard room is now one of the two dining rooms of Madrona Manor, where gourmet meals are served to guests and to the public. The cuisine is orchestrated by several chefs who use a brick oven, smokehouse, orchard and vegetable-herb garden to provide memorable meals. Having a restaurant in-house adds an unexpected luxury to this grand bed and breakfast estate.

MADRONA MANOR, 1001 Westside Road, Box 818, Healdsburg, CA 95448; (707) 433-4231; Carol and John Muir, owners; Todd Muir, resident chef, and Denice Fitzgerald, pastry chef, both graduates of California Culinary Academy. John Fitzgerald, resident landscape architect and Mark Muir, resident maintenance manager (all family). Eighteen rooms, all with private baths; five in manor and balance in carriage house and adjacent buildings. Rates: $75 to $125. Includes full breakfast in dining room or on outdoor terrace. Children welcome; manageable pets by arrangement; smoking allowed but guests are requested not to smoke in bed; Visa/MasterCard/American Express. Wheelchair access to one downstairs bedroom.

DIRECTIONS: from US-101, take the second Healdsburg exit. At the first stoplight, make a left onto Mill Street. In approximately ¾ of a mile the road turns to the left and the arched white gateway to the manor is straight ahead.

CAMELLIA INN

Simple grace and elegance

Built in 1869, the Camellia Inn is an early example of an Italianate Victorian building whose lines are exceptionally simple and graceful. Keeping the Victorian furnishings to a refreshing minimum allows the architecture to speak for itself. High ceilings, twin white marble fireplaces in two adjacent parlors, and tall, arched windows are all enhanced by natural light reflected off the salmon colored walls. Silk-screened wallpaper, a hand-crocheted bedspread, and satin pillows add just the right touches in the guest rooms.

Two of the rooms, Moon Glow and Demitasse, are in the main house and share a classic 1920s green-tiled bathroom. Moon Glow is named for the soft moonlight that shines through the cedar trees into the spacious room. Demitasse, overlooking an outdoor fishpond, is named for its coziness and charm. The remaining four rooms, located in a separate building, are reached by

The quiet elegance of the entrance hall, above, and the classic proportions of the building, right, give the 1869 home a sophisticated urban look.

crossing a small patio. A favorite room, once the original dining room of the home, and now called the Royalty Suite, has a massive maple tester bed brought from a castle in Scotland.

Camellia Inn is a wonderful place to visit in any season. On chilly mornings a fire in the breakfast room adds romance as well as warmth. In summer, you can sip a glass of wine under the shade trees near the large swimming pool.

A stay at the Camellia Inn often includes a tour of owners' Ray and Del Lewand's home-style winemaking facilities.

CAMELLIA INN, 211 North Street, Healdsburg, CA 95448; (707) 433-8182; Ray and Del Lewand, owners. Six rooms, four with private baths. Several with private entrances. Each furnished with period antiques. Rates: $40 to $65. Includes full breakfast of fresh fruit, homemade breads, and eggs. Guests are invited to join the hosts for wine and cheese in the evening. Children by special arrangement during the week; no pets; smoking in the parlors, but not in bedrooms; Visa/MasterCard. Swimming pool. Two blocks from town square. Over 40 wineries within seven miles and good fishing for steelhead not far away.

DIRECTIONS: from US-101 take the second Healdsburg exit. Proceed north for three blocks and turn right onto North Street.

OVERLEAF: *The Hop Kiln Winery at the Griffin Ranch Vineyards in Healdsburg was once an old hops-drying barn, and is now a National Historic Landmark. Eight varietal wines can be sampled in the tasting rooms.*

Angles, eaves, and arches define the upstairs rooms.

GRAPE LEAF INN

Chardonnay Suite, Pinot Noir Room

In what appears to be a small house of no particular architectural note, the playfulness of the Grape Leaf Inn comes as a surprise. It is hard to believe that there are seven bedrooms tucked into this house. The first floor is unadorned and cozy, with several overstuffed couches and a dining table snugly fitted into one room. But upstairs the Grape Leaf comes alive. The second floor has been totally remodeled, and four of the bedrooms have been built under the attic eaves.

Each of the upstairs rooms has two to four dormer windows to let in an abundance of light. The dramatic roof, dormers, and arches are accented with mirrors, stained-glass, and decorative wood, making the space whimsical and vibrant. Each room, named after a different grape, is decorated to match the grape's color. There is a rose-accented Gamay Room, a yellow and white Chardonnay Suite, and a Pinot Noir Room trimmed in purple.

Best of all is the attention given to the bathrooms. All four upstairs rooms have modern tiled baths, with large skylights over spacious whirlpool tub/showers for two. The prospect of bathing under a blue sky or a yellow moon is quite appealing.

GRAPE LEAF INN, 539 Johnson Street, Healdsburg, CA 95448; (707) 433-8140; Terry Sweet, owner. Kathy Cookson, hostess. Seven rooms, each with private bath. Three are traditional period rooms and four are remodeled to combine contemporary styles. Rates: $45 to $95. Includes full breakfast with homemade breads and egg dish. No children under twelve; no pets; smoking outside only; Visa/MasterCard. Downstairs rooms are wheelchair accessible.

DIRECTIONS: take second Healdsburg exit and proceed on Healdsburg Av. Take a right onto Grant St. and the Grape Leaf is two blocks on the right at the corner of Johnson and Grant.

THE OLD CROCKER INN

A true western flavor

After crossing the Russian River there is a mile-long drive up through the hills to the Old Crocker Inn. With a spectacular view of the Sonoma Valley, the inn's five acres are bounded by quarter horses grazing in nearby pastures and cactus-studded open fields. Secluded and lodgelike, the inn has a true western flavor.

Five ample guest rooms in the main building surround an inner courtyard. With twelve-foot ceilings and large, glass-paned double doors, the rooms open out on a spacious railed veranda that encircles the building.

Overlooking the valley is a dramatic circular dining room, paneled in California tan oak and Hawaiian Kauri wood. A full country breakfast is served, and the professional kitchen is ready to cater an occasional wedding. It will be hard to leave the wonderful pool to explore the wineries nearby.

THE OLD CROCKER INN, 26532 River Road, Cloverdale, CA 95425; (707) 894-3911; Deborah and Edward Lyons, hosts. German spoken fluently. Ten rooms with private baths, five in main lodge and five in various private and semi-private adjacent buildings. Rates: $50 to $70. Includes a full country breakfast. Children allowed in separate cottages; no pets; Visa/MasterCard. Dog, several cats, a horse and at least five chickens in residence.

DIRECTIONS: from US-101 north: MAY THROUGH NOVEMBER: exit at Asti. Bear right for 100 feet and take Asti Rd. to the right. Proceed ¼ mile and take a left onto Washington School Rd. Cross Russian River. The road takes a severe turn to the left, and in ¼ mile, look for the sign to Crocker. Proceed up the hill for about a mile. DECEMBER THROUGH APRIL: exit in Cloverdale and turn right onto First St. Cross Russian River and bear right at the Y in the road onto River Rd. Follow about 3½ miles and turn left at the sign.

The rustic lodge overlooks the Russian River Valley and Sonoma vineyards.

TOLL HOUSE INN

A fascinating hostess

Originally spoken by the young men of this valley from 1880 to 1920, Boontling is the jargon you'll hear in this little town. Basically a vocabulary of one thousand words, the language provided menfolk with a private tongue, which, as evidenced by some of the puzzling signs you'll see, is enjoying a renaissance. "Horn of zeese for the applehead" means ordering a cup of coffee for your girl.

A visitor does not have to speak Boontling to feel at home at Bev Nesbitt's Toll House Inn. Because Bev is so adept at anticipating needs, her guests need little in the way of vocabulary except plenty of thank-yous. She is gracious and kind, with the virtues of an aunt with the knack for helping relatives relax and enjoy themselves. Her interesting and varied background, which includes everything from cattle ranching, trucking, and commercial fishing to modeling and surfing makes her a fascinating woman.

Fabulous breakfasts are served up in a sunny dining room, and gourmet dinners are available by reservation. The rooms are large, inviting, and furnished in stylish good taste. There is a wonderful patio, hot tub, and attractive perennial garden.

TOLL HOUSE INN, P.O. Box 268, 15301 Highway 253, Boonville, CA 95415; (707) 895-3630; Beverly Nesbitt, hostess. Spanish and Italian spoken. Four rooms, two suites with private baths and fireplaces. Rates: $60 to $86. Includes a full breakfast with fresh fruits, omelets, biscuits or muffins. Complimentary wine in each room. Children over twelve; no pets; no credit cards. Raley the dog and Aimee the cat in residence. Located in a secluded valley in the heart of Mendocino wine country.

DIRECTIONS: from San Francisco take US-101 North to Rte. 253 west, which is 11 miles south of Ukiah. From Boonville take Rte. 128 south and Rte. 253 east for 6 miles.

HOPE-BOSWORTH HOPE-MERRILL

Two restored homes reflect different periods

Careful research and painstaking attention to detail by innkeepers Bob and Rosalie Hope are evident throughout their Hope-Merrill and Hope-Bosworth homes. The houses, across from each other on Geyserville's main street, reflect different periods and therefore differing styles and moods.

Hope-Merrill, built around the 1880s, is an Eastlake and Stick Victorian with formal lines. The interior is similar in design, with elegant wainscoting, a carved banister on a curved stairway, and high graceful windows. The home has been awarded accolades for its authentic décor, which includes lovely period antiques, a Victorian dollhouse, a fire screen embroidered with calla lilies, Parrish lithographs, and bountiful displays of Victorian memorabilia, including a glass case of beaded handbags.

Hope-Bosworth, built in 1904, is a "pattern-book house," built from plans selected and ordered from catalogues offering the popular contemporary styles of the day. It is predictably simpler in design and mood. The building is more square, and the rooms are symmetrical; the staircase climbs at utilitarian right angles. With pale oak and wicker furnishings and patterned wallpapers, the overall décor is less ceremonious, giving a country feeling to the house. Tall palm trees, more than seventy feet high, stand at the entrance to Hope-Bosworth, and a white picket fence encloses the yard.

The houses provide an interesting and educational glimpse into bygone eras that suited two particular life-styles. Today, either provides a lovely base from which to explore the wineries and recreational activities of the Russian River and surrounding countryside.

HOPE-BOSWORTH and HOPE-MERRILL, 21238 Geyserville Ave., Geyserville, CA 95441; (707) 857-3356; Bob & Rosalie Hope, owners. Five rooms in each house. Private, half, and shared baths. Rates: $45 to $60. Includes a continental breakfast with fruits and breads. No children; no pets; smoking only in designated areas and not in bedrooms; Visa/MasterCard/American Express. Catered dinners by advance reservation.

DIRECTIONS: from US-101, exit at Geyserville; the houses are across the street from one another on the main street of Geyserville.

Elegantly restored guest rooms: in the Hope-Merrill, left, and the Hope-Bosworth, above.

NORTHERN CALIFORNIA

THE PELICAN INN

Shakespeare could have slept here

Perfectly natural in its wooded seaside setting, this sixteenth-century-style English country manor exudes the hospitality and comfort of the old English pub and inn. A fire blazes on the full hearth, and folks are gathered with mugs of ale or cups of mulled wine cheering players at the dart board. Meat pies and Scotch eggs are served on long, candlelit wooden tables. And as the English might say, there is good fellowship in plentiful proportions.

Upstairs are six rooms, all continuing the sixteenth-century theme. Canopied beds, lovely antiques, and recessed leaded windows enhance the feeling of taking a step back in time. There is even a step stool to help you get into the high old bed.

Never has a 400-year-old inn, restaurant, and pub been so authentically replicated. It is the realization of one man's dream, Charles Felix, who wanted to resurrect a family hotel in Surrey that went back five generations. Built in 1977, and twenty minutes from San Francisco, the Pelican is indeed in another world. The fascination and appeal of the Pelican are perhaps best reflected by the need to reserve a weekend six months in advance.

THE PELICAN INN, Muir Beach, CA 94965; (415) 383-6000; Charles and Brenda Felix, publicans; Cece Berlinger, reservations manager. Six rooms, each with private bath and shower. Queen-size beds and half testers in each very English room. Rates: $90. Includes a hearty English breakfast of eggs, bangers (English pork sausages), fruit, and broiled tomatoes. Children are allowed and rollaway beds are available; no pets; Visa/MasterCard. A cat, Sheba, a Dachshund named Banger, and a great Dane named Dekan are in residence.

DIRECTIONS: twenty minutes from Golden Gate Bridge on Rte. 1. From US-101, take Stinson Beach/Highway 1 exit and stay to the left.

Left, Marin County California coastline—a forever changing drama. Above is the Pelican Inn, just a few miles north.

BLACKTHORNE INN

A magical place

The Blackthorne is a product of the late sixties and early seventies, when people were building adventurous, nonconformist dream houses. Located in a canyon near Point Reyes National Seashore, it is a stunning example of an imaginative person's nontraditional approaches to living space. The Blackthorne, in fact, looks like an elegant treehouse.

Endlessly fascinating with its multiple levels, the Blackthorne is a series of interconnecting decks, handcrafted details, stained-glass windows, skylights—and a firepole for the limber to get from one level to another. There is a large stone hearth, laid by the Blackthorne's owner.

A four-story spiral staircase leads to an octagonal room in the building's tower. Known as the Eagle's Nest, the room has windows on every side and can also be reached by a forty-foot catwalk that connects with the highest of four decks. A thick blue carpet and Japanese futon are the only furnishings, making the treetops and sky the true decorative elements.

Perfect for the young at heart, the Blackthorne is one of the most romantic of the bed and breakfasts. There is every convenience here, including modern shared bathrooms, full hearty breakfasts, and the opportunity to try side-by-side tubs on a redwood deck. The Blackthorne is magical.

BLACKTHORNE INN, P.O. Box 712, Inverness, CA 94937; (415) 663-8621; Bill Wigert, owner; Susan and Bill Hemphill, managers. Five rooms with shared baths. Rates: $50 to $90. Includes light and healthy continental breakfast of fruits, cereals, yogurt, and breads. Children by arrangement; no pets; Visa/MasterCard. Pt. Reyes National Seashore nearby with miles of hiking trails and beautiful seashore.

DIRECTIONS: take US-101 to Sir Francis Drake Blvd. exit and proceed west to Olema. Take a right turn onto Rte. 1. Proceed about two miles and make a left turn towards Inverness. Go 1 mile and take a left onto Vallejo just before Perry's Inverness Park Grocery.

Left above, the Eagle's Nest, the most romantic, magical room on the coast.

ELK COVE INN

For a romantic weekend by the sea

Perched strategically on a bluff overlooking the powerful Pacific and one of its sheltered coves, Elk Cove Inn is the perfect destination for a romantic weekend by the sea. The main house is a Victorian cottage that contains several bedrooms, a dining room, a living room with working fireplace, and a library. A short distance away, attached by a walkway, a separate redwood structure houses several comfortable bedrooms with beamed ceilings. Just past the inn's old-fashioned flower garden, a staircase to the beach beckons.

Innkeeper Hildrun-Uta Triebess has welcomed guests into her home for two decades. A spirited hostess, she is well known for her talent in the kitchen. Breakfast is full and generous and often includes German egg cakes or omelets. For the convenience and delight of her guests, as well as the occasional outsider, Hildrun-Uta serves a multicourse continental dinner, included in the price of the stay. Guests might enjoy coq au vin blanc, salmon in sour cream, or poached meatballs in lemon-caper sauce.

ELK COVE INN, Highway One, P.O. Box 367, Elk, CA 95432; (707) 877-3321; Hildrun-Uta Triebess, hostess. German, French, Spanish, Italian spoken. Four rooms in main house and five rooms in guest house. All rooms with spectacular ocean views. Rates: weekends $98 to $148 double; weekdays $46 to $82 double. Includes a full breakfast of German egg cakes or omelets and a gourmet German or French dinner of several courses. Children over twelve; no pets; Visa/MasterCard. Baasco is a friendly pygmy goat in residence.

DIRECTIONS: located on Rte. 1, 15 miles south of Mendocino. From US-101 north exit at Cloverdale and take Rte. 128 west to the coast and go five miles south on Rte. 1.

A stone's throw from a dramatic beach.

Left, an incredible view adds to the pleasure of the hot tub. The elaborate bed, above, was used in the movie
Wuthering Heights.

THE OLD MILANO HOTEL

Spectacular views of the ocean

Built in 1905 near cliff-hanging railroad tracks, this old hotel offers spectacular views. Though no longer part of the scene, the railroad is remembered. The owners have bought a caboose, placed it in their woods, and furnished it to perfection for the railfan. Formerly used by the North Pacific Coast Railroad, it has a guest suite for two, with kitchenette and observation cupola.

The hotel's six grand guest rooms overlook the ocean, and are furnished with antique armoires and curious beds, including an oak sleigh bed. Pale green floral William Morris wallpaper distinguishes the lavish, plushly furnished formal parlor. Stones collected from local beaches were used to make a large fireplace in an adjacent parlor, where wine from the hotel's extensive collection of Northern California wines is served in the evenings.

An additional option for guests is the white clapboard Passion Vine Cottage, located on the hotel grounds. Covered in salmon-colored passion flowers, it is fitted with a sleeping loft, sitting room, and small kitchen.

THE OLD MILANO HOTEL, 38300 Highway 1, Gualala, CA 95445; (707) 884-3256; Judith Fisher, hostess. Nine rooms, including a Caboose, a cottage, and remarkable suite with a private sitting room overlooking the ocean. Private and shared baths. Open all year, but weekends only from Thanksgiving to April 1. Rates: $60 to $120. Includes continental breakfast. No children; no pets; no smoking in the house. Visa/MasterCard/American Express. Hot tub. Massages available by certified practitioner. Excellent dining at nearby St. Orres.

DIRECTIONS: on Rte. 1 one mile north of Gualala; the entrance to the hotel is on the left.

A unique guest room.

WHALE WATCH INN

Gray whale vantage point

At the Whale Watch Inn, natural beauty and refreshing salt sea breezes vanquish the stress and tension of everyday life. The inn is a complex of contemporary buildings designed so that every room commands a sweeping view of the southern Mendocino coastline. Besides the vistas, the flicker of firelight in each guest's chamber creates a romantic atmosphere in the cool of the evening. If guests desire to remain in a private world of their own, breakfast is delivered to the door each morning. Those in a more gregarious mood gather for their morning meal in front of a circular fireplace in the hexagonal Whale Watch Room. A light and sustaining fare of fruits, breads, yogurt, and cheeses starts the day off right.

The weather pattern along this patch of coast is atypical. Known as "the banana belt," the Gualala area is free from the thick fogs that frequently blanket much of the northern coast of California. The result is an unparalleled vantage point on the pathway of the migrating gray whales that travel along the coast from winter to spring.

WHALE WATCH INN BY THE SEA, 35100 Highway 1, Gualala, CA 95445; (707) 884-3667; Irene & Enoch Stewart, owners; Aurora Hayes, hostess. Fourteen rooms in three contemporary buildings, each with private bath, several with full kitchens and fireplaces, several with private decks, suites, and spas. Rates: $75 to $135. Includes continental breakfast of fresh fruits, fresh breads, cheese or yogurt. No children; no pets; no smoking; Visa/ MasterCard. Stairs to private sheltered beach.

DIRECTIONS: from US-101 at Petaluma exit, turn left onto Washington Street. Take Rte. 1 north from Valley Ford.

Left, the inn looks out on a beautiful shoreline. Above, a unique weathervane tells the story of this inn.

The perfect bed and breakfast cabin for those with an adventurous spirit.

HOWARD CREEK RANCH

Rural retreat by the sea

Bordered by the vast Pacific Ocean and set in a secluded valley surrounded by lush green farm country, Howard Creek Ranch is perfect for those who cannot decide whether to vacation in the country or stop by the sea. The main complex here comprises two back-to-back New England-style farmhouses furnished in true country fashion, with a fireplace, overstuffed furniture, and the unexpected—like a moose head over the piano. One of the guest rooms has its own kitchen and private balcony. With a loft bed under a skylight, the other guest room looks out on the stars.

For those who like to rough it, there's the hull of a fishing boat that has somehow grown into a cabin complete with a galley kitchen, patchwork-quilt-covered bed, and a large picture window overlooking the creek. For those even more adventurous, another rustic cabin provides cold running water and a wood-burning stove.

Howard Creek Ranch provides the opportunity for beachcombing, swimming in a fresh-water creek, and bike riding along the beach—all offered up with country-style hospitality.

HOWARD CREEK RANCH, P.O. Box 121, Westport CA 95488; (707) 964-6725; Sunny and Sally Lasselle-Griggs, owners; Noemi Botteselle, housekeeper. German, Dutch, French, Italian spoken. Three rooms in main house with shared baths, plus boat house, and rustic cabin. Rates: $35 to $65. Includes a hearty ranch breakfast of hotcakes, eggs, bacon or sausage. Children and pets often welcome by previous arrangement; no credit cards. Swimming pool filled with fresh creek water. Hot tub and sauna heated by wood. Massage by reservation.

DIRECTIONS: located on Rte. 1, three miles north of Westport. Entrance is by milepost 80.49. Turn east and bear left and you'll see big white farmhouse.

Left, Victoriana and exquisite craftsmanship combine to create a striking redwood exterior. Above, Christi and Mark Carter share a sense of history as they stand in front of their spectacular house.

THE CARTER HOUSE

Re-creation of an earthquake casualty

Mark Carter found his dream house in a book of Victorian architecture at a friend's antiques store. The original house in San Francisco, destroyed in the earthquake of 1906, had been designed in 1884 by Samuel and Joseph Newson, who were also the architects of Eureka's famous Carson Mansion. Using the Newson's plans, Mark, with the help of several young assistants, re-created the house a century later. It took him sixteen months to complete his masterpiece of modern-day craftsmanship.

Extraordinarily fine antiques grace the parlors and dining room, but unlike Victorian homes, it has no dark or somber interior. White walls and marble floors blend with natural polished oak and redwood wainscoting, making all of the rooms bright and open. Contemporary paintings and graphics by local artists hang throughout the house. These, along with porcelain and ceramic pieces, are for sale in the Carters' first-floor art gallery. Woven baskets filled with potted mums are everywhere.

Breakfasts are prepared by Christi Carter, who formerly owned a restaurant and ice cream parlor. Pear, Grand Marnier, and almond phyllo tarts are not beyond her delectable repertoire.

Hospitality comes easily to the Carters, who serve cocktails and hors d'oeuvres in the evening, and cordials, tea, and cookies as a late-night snack. They are delighted to tell you about nearby Old Town, which is an impressive restoration of the surrounding waterfront, and to share with you their enthusiasm for the splendors of Eureka, of which they are so prominently a part.

THE CARTER HOUSE, Third & L Streets, Eureka, CA 95501; (707) 445-1390; Mark and Christi Carter, hosts. Seven rooms, private and shared baths. Wheelchair access to ground floor rooms. Rates $35 to $120. Includes an elegant, full breakfast of fresh fruit, an egg dish, muffins, and delicate pastries. Cordials in the afternoon, tea or coffee and homemade treats in the evening. Business rates mid-week: $35 to $65, single with continental breakfast. No children or pets; smoking on main floor, but not in rooms; Visa/MasterCard.

DIRECTIONS: take 101 into North Eureka and go west on L Street.

This Carpenter Gothic house is filled with antiques and treasures collected over a lifetime.

SHAW HOUSE INN

A superb example of Carpenter Gothic

The bed in Shaw House Inn's Honeymoon Suite is the same bed used by local couples a hundred years ago who were married by Seth Shaw, Justice of the Peace and founder of Ferndale. Seth Lewis Shaw's home, begun in 1854 and completed in 1866, has endured as a remarkable contribution to the historical integrity of the area. The elaborate Victorian Gothic Revival house of steep gables, recessed porches, intricate gingerbread trim, and balconies is set along the creek that Shaw first navigated into this valley. Built on land he cleared of overgrown ferns, the house is a tribute to his pioneering spirit and signaled the beginning of farming in this community.

The house was always open to visitors and travelers in Shaw's time, and innkeeper Velna Polizza (formerly an antiques dealer) shares this tradition. Her dedication to the preservation of this house and her high regard for the historical renaissance in Ferndale are everywhere evident in her restoration of the home to its previous splendor. The formal parlor, dining room, and bedrooms echo the refinements of an earlier era. She has added, as well, her lifelong collection of fine glass, art, china, and other antiques, including some of museum quality.

SHAW HOUSE INN, 703 Main Street, Ferndale, CA 95536; (707) 786-9958; Velna Polizza, owner. Five rooms, private and shared baths. Rates: $45 to $75. Includes full breakfast of fresh fruit compote, egg dish, bread. Children sufficiently responsible to take their own rooms are welcome; no pets; smoking on outside balconies and porches only; no credit cards. Lady Amber Ashley is cat in residence.

DIRECTIONS: from US-101, exit at Ferndale. Proceed about 5 miles and the sign for Shaw House is on the right.

*Left, the garden-like bathroom, decorated with imported French floral wallpaper.
The inn, above, is a gingerbread classic, and the topiary gardens, OVERLEAF, add to the fantasy.*

GINGERBREAD MANSION

Everything adds to the fantasy

Years ago, when the town wanted to tear it down, two gentlemen bought this house. They spent eighteen years restoring it, and one of them, a landscape gardener, created the beautiful and unusual topiary, something rarely seen in this country.

A spectacular peach and yellow high-Victorian, the Gingerbread Mansion has delicate woodwork around turrets, gables, tower, and porches. Two camellia bushes, shaped into trees, stand guard in front of the house and add to the fantasy. Called the "Butterfat Palaces of Cream City," houses like this one were built for Ferndale's successful dairy farmers.

Wendy Hatfield and Ken Torbert bought the mansion two years ago and turned it into a bed and breakfast. The furnishings are eclectic. Pieces include Victorian settees, Eastlake tables, and carved French armoires, as well as a variety of patterned wallpapers, a bird's-eye maple fireplace, Oriental carpets, and wood-burning Franklin stoves.

Each day, one of a variety of delicious breads—lemon, pumpkin, or cranberry-apple—is served for breakfast, and Wendy's bran muffins are becoming famous.

Little extras add personal warmth to the elegance. Turned-down beds, bathrobes, early-morning coffee or tea, vintage bicycles for exploring back roads into canyons, and boots and umbrellas if it rains are amenities appreciated by guests who stop here.

THE GINGERBREAD MANSION, 400 Berding Street, Ferndale, CA 95536; (707) 786-4000; Wendy Hatfield and Ken Torbert, hosts. Fluent in Spanish and Portuguese with some French and Japanese. Four rooms, shared baths and two with sinks in the room. Rates: $45 to $65. Includes a generous continental breakfast of fresh fruit platter, selection of fruit breads and local cheeses. Sherry in the evening and sweets at bedtime. Children ten and over welcome; no pets; no smoking permitted in the house, but there is a veranda off the second floor with chairs, lap blanket, and ashtrays to accommodate smokers; Visa/MasterCard.

DIRECTIONS: from US-101, exit at Ferndale. Proceed about five miles into town and turn left onto Brown Street at the Bank of America. The house is ahead on the left one block.

THE PLOUGH AND THE STARS COUNTRY INN

A lighthearted, casual atmosphere

Hosts Melissa and Bill Hans.

When Melissa and Bill Hans discovered a century-old farmhouse in the far reaches of Humboldt County, they visualized a dream come true. Combining Bill's love for the country with Melissa's professional background in food and restaurant management, they created a charming rural inn whose warm hospitality typifies bed and breakfast travel. The inn is especially snug and congenial on cool and misty days when guests can warm themselves by the fire blazing in the hearth. And for sunny days there is a spacious patio.

After a breakfast of Melissa's fresh-baked breads and succulent fruit topped with a generous dollop of *crème fraîche*, visitors may enjoy a game of croquet on the lawn or a drive into Arcata. There are shops, restaurants, and a movie theater, where for two dollars you can catch a double feature of classic films.

THE PLOUGH AND THE STARS COUNTRY INN, 1800 27th Street, Arcata, CA 95521; (707) 822-8236; Bill and Melissa Hans, hosts. Five rooms with shared baths. Upstairs sitting room. Rates: $35 to $57. Winter rates discounted. Includes a full continental breakfast of strawberries and *crème fraîche* in season and English muffins or toast and sweet bread. Eggs and bacon prepared for slight additional charge. Children over twelve; outdoor pets by arrangement, but will need to get along with friendly black Labrador, Hannah, and three cats; no credit cards. Wheelchair access to ground-floor room.

DIRECTIONS: on US-101 north, exit at Somoa Blvd. Loop up over freeway heading West for about ½ a mile. Take a right onto K St. Continue on K St., which bends to the left and becomes Alliance Rd., and take a left onto 27th St. The sign and the inn are ³⁄₁₀ of a mile on the right.

Built in the 1860s in the flatlands of scenic Humboldt County.

OREGON

CLIFF HARBOR HOUSE

Where nature restores your spirit

There is no coastline in North America that compares with Oregon's expansive beaches, roaring surf, and buffeting winds. Here nature's power is revealed in the most elemental way. You can feel its forces reenergizing you.

Respite from the elements is offered by Cliff Harbor Guest House, overlooking the spectacular rocks and surf of Bandon beach in southern Oregon. You can watch the foaming breakers, the cormorants, the puffins from a cushioned window seat while Luciano Pavarotti's voice swells in the background from the living room stereo.

Cliff Harbor's unbelievably beautiful setting constantly renews the spirit. Doris and Bill Duncan knew that when they built their private retreat. Guests are welcomed and can stay in two comfortably modern redwood suites. The largest has a freestanding fireplace, a full kitchen, a dressing table, two double beds, and a view of the west, where most evenings one can see the glorious colors of the setting sun sinking into the Pacific Ocean. The hospitality of the Duncans allows fortunate guests to experience the exhilarating, wild beauty of the Oregon coast from a safe haven.

CLIFF HARBOR GUEST HOUSE, P.O. Box 769, Bandon, OR 97411; (503) 347-3956, 344-4132; Doris and Bill Duncan, hosts. Two spacious, modern suites, both with private entrances and wheelchair access, one with fireplace and kitchen. Rates: $45 to $52 double. Slightly less during the winter. Includes a wonderful full breakfast with rolls or cranberry bread, fluffy omelets or eggs, and bacon. Children welcome; no pets; no credit cards. The old section of Bandon is experiencing a renaissance, offering a tasteful selection of galleries, shops, and natural food restaurants.
DIRECTIONS: provided upon reservation confirmation.

Left, sea grass covers the dunes behind the inn, which overlooks the scenic wonder of Bandon beach, above. OVERLEAF: *view of the inn, the beach, and the colorful gorse, or Irish furze, brought from Bandon, Ireland, by the town's founder, Lord Bennet.*

JOHNSON HOUSE

Turn-of-the-century charm

Built in 1892, this is purported to be the oldest house in Florence. Much of its original wooden trim and detailing remain intact. Although the interior has undergone major restoration, the square symmetrical parlor and dining room have been retained.

Turn-of-the-century furnishings throughout, coupled with accents of lace, freshly cut flowers, and old sepia portraits, add to the house's charm. Included in the stay is a full breakfast of fresh fruits with cream, omelets, an assortment of breads, or Grand Marnier French toast.

Once a prosperous logging town, today Florence is a bustling summertime tourist town, with an expanse of oceanside sand dunes for wonderful beachcombing.

JOHNSON HOUSE, 216 Maple Street, P.O. Box 1892, Florence, OR 97439; (503) 997-8000; Jayne and Ronald Fraese, owners; Jeff Swanson, manager. French spoken by the Fraeses. Four rooms, shared baths. Rates: $34. Includes a full breakfast. No children under fourteen; no pets; no smoking; no credit cards.

DIRECTIONS: from US-101, turn west onto Maple street approximately 2 blocks north of the bridge over the Siuslaw River.

The Craftsman cottage inn is a short walk from the Shakespearian Festival Theater, right.

CHANTICLEER BED & BREAKFAST INN

Salmon quiche or cheese blintzes?

An exterior view of Jim and Nancy Beaver's Chanticleer Bed and Breakfast Inn reveals a simple and well-proportioned Craftsman bungalow whose strength of character derives from the softly hued porch constructed of native river stone. Entering the inn, one is captivated by its country-French interior.

The six guest bedrooms are a refreshing and sprightly mix of pastel wall coverings, coordinated floral sheets and puffy down comforters, fresh flowers, and rich carpeting. In the first-floor living room, Nancy's lustrous Haviland china collection is displayed in a glass case.

Each morning Jim and Nancy serve an especially generous and delicious breakfast in the dining room, whose windows open onto the foothills of the Cascade Mountains.

Ashland is justly famous for its high-quality Shakespeare festival, which runs year-round. Each season, the festival stages four to six Shakespeare plays as well as American classics and one original play.

CHANTICLEER BED & BREAKFAST INN, 120 Gresham Street, Ashland, OR 97520; (505) 482-1919; Jim and Nancy Beaver, hosts. Six rooms, each with private bath. Decorated in a fresh French country style. Rates: $59. Winter discount. Includes full breakfast with fruit course, and main entrée of baked eggs, salmon quiche, or cheese blinzes, coffee cake or croissant. Children welcome; no pets; no smoking in bedrooms; no credit cards.

DIRECTIONS: from the south on I-5 take Siskiyou Av. exit and turn left on Third St. (just after sign for public library). Proceed ½ block on 3rd which becomes Gresham.

LIVINGSTON MANSION

The romance of history

Built high on a rise overlooking the foothills of the Siskiyou Mountains and the valley of the Rouge River, Livingston Mansion affords a spectacular view of Jacksonville and the surrounding terrain. From the cool depths of its western-style, paneled living room, where a fire crackles on the massive stone hearth, to the contemporary, sun-spangled swimming pool, visitors feel the romantic heritage of a historic locale.

Gold was discovered in the area in 1852, and the village attracted wealth and commerce. For a time, Jacksonville was the largest town in southern Oregon. Designated a National Historic District, today it is a monument to western history. Visitors enjoy strolling through the charming streets, where meticulously restored buildings echo the past.

LIVINGSTON MANSION, 4132 Livingston Road, P.O. Box 1476, Jacksonville, OR 97530; (503) 899-7107; Wally and Sherry Lossing, hosts. Five rooms, three with private baths. Rates: $45 to $75. Includes full breakfast that often includes fresh fruit and ice cream, eggs Benedict or crêpes, breads and "breakfast cookies." Business rates. Families welcome, but small children not encouraged; no pets; smoking permitted in the living room and on outside patio only; Visa/MasterCard. Sheba is the dog in residence. Swimming pool and small pond.

DIRECTIONS: from I-5 take the Medford exit and proceed west on Rte. 238. Go through Jacksonville and take a right onto North Oregon St. Continue about a mile to Livingston, take a left, and follow to the top of the hill.

CAMPUS COTTAGE

Unpretentious charm near Fraternity Row

Campus Cottage is a cozy frame bungalow tucked along the border of the University of Oregon's beautiful campus. Situated among the sprawling structures of Fraternity Row, the inn is ideally located for visitors to the university and is minutes away from downtown Eugene.

Innkeeper Ursula Bates, herself an experienced traveler, waxes enthusiastic about the pleasures of bed and breakfast inns. Committed to starting each day with a nourishing meal, she serves guests a variety of breakfast foods, from egg dishes and fresh fruits to hot breads and beverages. Ursula is a knowledgeable guide to her city and is especially proud of the new Hult Center for the Performing Arts, the fine selection of French restaurants, and the Fifth Street Public Market, which is Eugene's answer to San Francisco's Ghirardelli Square.

CAMPUS COTTAGE, 1136 East 19th Avenue, Eugene, OR 97403; (503) 342-5346; Ursula Bates, owner. Two rooms currently. Rates: $55 to $65. Includes a full, hearty breakfast with a variety of egg dishes, fresh fruits. Older children only; no pets; no credit cards. Gus, the cat, and Annie, the dog, in residence.

DIRECTIONS: from the south on I-5, exit at 192 which becomes Franklin Blvd. Take a left at the third light onto Agate St., following signs to the University of Oregon. Turn right onto 19th St. and go 3½ blocks.

MADISON INN

A family affair

Aided by six offspring who are responsible for everything from bookkeeping to cooking, Kathryn Brandeis has created an open and relaxing guest house in her gracious, gabled home.

Perhaps the main reason for the genial atmosphere at the Madison Inn is Kathryn's genius with people. Explains eldest son Matthew: "Mom is incredible. She knows a little something about almost everything and can always spur interesting conversation around the breakfast table."

The spectacular woodwork, moldings, and architectural detail of the house warrant its entry on the National Historic Register.

Located across from a quiet park, the Madison Inn is convenient to both Oregon State University and downtown Corvallis. But the real attraction of the inn is the warmth and hospitality of the Brandeis clan.

MADISON INN, 660 Madison, Corvallis, OR 97330; (503) 757-1274; Kathryn Brandeis, owner; Paige, Matthew, Honore, Mike, Shannon, and Kathleen Brandeis, deputy hosts. Spanish and French spoken. Five rooms, one with private bath, the remaining four rooms sharing two baths. Rate: $40. Includes full breakfast of baked eggs, English muffins, and blended fruit juices. Children welcome; no pets; Raggs is the household dog.

DIRECTIONS: from I-5, take the Corvallis-Oregon State exit. Go west ten miles, cross over bridge and take a left onto 6th. Go three blocks, take a right onto Madison, and continue to 7th.

Beautifully preserved woodwork reflects the character of this 1903 Queen Anne.

Built high on the rocky shore overlooking this inlet, Channel House commands a magnificent view of all nautical comings-and-goings. A modern, shingled structure, the inn was designed with the sea in mind, and the most desirable accommodations are those that face the water. With sliding glass doors that open onto private balconies, these rooms make guests feel as if they have set to sea. Two of the large oceanfront suites, equipped with full kitchens, working fireplaces, and whirlpool baths, are perfect for two couples traveling together.

Breakfast can be enjoyed in the first-floor restaurant, decorated with an array of antique brass ships' fittings, or in the privacy of one's room. In the restaurant, a CB radio picks up fishing news from the nearby boats. Charter boats, equipped for a day of serious fishing or for a pleasure cruise, are available at the harbor.

CHANNEL HOUSE

Endless
nautical views

Carved by nature from the rugged Oregon coastline, Depoe Bay is a calm and picturesque body of water favored by sport and commercial fishermen alike. However, navigators pay their dues in the channel that connects the bay to the sea. Nicknamed "The Jaws," it is a treacherous inlet that commands the respect of the most stalwart old salt.

CHANNEL HOUSE, P.O. Box 49, Depoe Bay, OR 97341; (503) 765-2140; Paul Schwabe, owner. Seven rooms, each with private bath, two of which are large oceanfront suites with full kitchens, fireplaces and whirlpools. Rates: $30 to $95. Includes full continental breakfast. Children are welcome, as are well-behaved pets by previous arrangement.

DIRECTIONS: located on the coast between Newport and Lincoln. Turn west at supermarket onto Ellingson St., just south of the bridge over Depoe Bay.

Perched right on the ocean, you can have breakfast in your room and look at the view. OVERLEAF: *View from the inn of Depoe Bay, a real Oregon coastal town.*

WASHINGTON

INN OF THE WHITE SALMON

Where good taste prevails

This is the place to come for breakfast and to stay several extra days—that is, if you want to taste everything. Both pastry chef and innkeeper, Loretta Hopper serves more than forty different items daily. Pastries, cakes, breads, and tarts are freshly baked with an assist from two other bakers, and there are orange cream-cheese rolls, pear frangipane, cinnamon toast, flan, Danish bread dough with an almond paste filling, and tart Mirabelle with kirsch-soaked prunes. All are beautiful to behold and incredibly delicious. Since there are six different egg dishes in addition to everything else, it is impossible to try everything at even two or three breakfasts.

Some of the 42 breakfast treats.

INN OF THE WHITE SALMON, 172 W. Jewett, White Salmon, WA 98672; (509) 493-2335; Loretta and Bill Hopper, owners. Patricia White, manager. Nineteen rooms, each with private bath, furnished with period antiques in two-story 1930s brick building. Rates: $54.95 to $68.95. Includes an extraordinary breakfast of fresh pastries and gourmet egg dishes. Well-supervised children welcome; no pets; smoking permitted but not in dining room; Visa/MasterCard/American Express. Hot tub. Located in the fabulously beautiful Columbia River gorge.

DIRECTIONS: east of Portland on I-84, for 64 miles to exit 64. Follow signs to White Salmon; the inn is towards the end of town on the right.

The Multnomah Falls, left, at 620 feet the highest in Oregon. Above, Loretta Hopper, hostess and pastry chef.

Modeled after a 15th-century English inn, and reproduced in authentic detail.

THE SWAN INN

Sample the fifteenth century

After spending their honeymoon at the Crown Inn of Chiddingfold, Surrey, England, and falling in love with it, Richard and Jeri Bain decided to re-create it. Nine years ago, they built this fifteenth-century English Tudor inn on an island of farmhouses. Set back in the woods at the end of a long driveway, the Swan Inn is startling to come upon.

After drawing up plans, the Bains worked with Australian Peter Crocker, a local contractor who was familiar with Tudor architecture. Cedar beam construction dating back a thousand years, leaded and stained-glass windows imported from abroad, and rustic old iron hardware all help to duplicate an authentic fifteenth-century inn. Crossing the threshold, one finds an entrance paved with old bricks, a 1790 English clock, and a Jacobean table from the 1600s.

Richard Bain is a dedicated preindustrialist, fascinated with the literature, philosophy, and life-styles of the fourteenth, fifteenth, and sixteenth centuries. The Swan Inn is filled with objects he has collected, including brass rubbings of a 1451 Flemish knight, a chest carved in 1606, a flintlock British musket dating from 1798, dozens of horse brasses, and an impressive array of other antique furnishings and treasures. Upstairs in a guest room, there is an oval mirror recessed into the foot of an ornate bed, which Richard explains was used by ladies to check their hemlines.

Jeri Bain is a published modern poet. Richard teasingly describes her as "the only member of the family in the twentieth century," even though

A chest carved in 1606 in Elizabethan England.

he is a consulting engineer when not in pursuit of history. Their youngest daughter, Margie, provides a tour of the family farm and introduces the cows, Tillie and Roxanne, the horses, Merry and Chance, and a pony named Rainbow. There are also ducks, geese, thirteen laying hens, five roosters, and a friendly boxer named Biscuit. In the barn, built by Richard, with timbers cut with an antique hewing ax, there are several vintage buggies ready to harness to the horses should you want a ride.

Nature in all its magnificence provides an idyllic setting for the Swan Inn—a special destination.

THE SWAN INN, Route 5, Box 454, Vashon, Vashon Island, WA 98070; (206) 463-3388; Jeri and Richard Bain, owners. Three rooms decorated in 15th- to 18th-century English furnishings with either a private or shared bath. Rates: $45 to $55. Includes an expanded continental breakfast week-days and a full breakfast weekends. Children over eight; no pets; Visa/MasterCard. Family bicycles are happily loaned, hiking trails go through surrounding woods, and the beach is 15 minutes away. Pool, tennis, and 9-hole golf course nearby.

DIRECTIONS: Vashon Island is a 15-minute ferry ride from West Seattle. From I-5, follow signs for Vashon Ferry which leaves from Fauntleroy Way. Take the main road to Vashon from either ferry dock, turn west at the stop light and follow Bank Road (SW 176th street). Watch for a blue mailbox No. 454 and "Swan Inn" sign.

A guest room, above, and hosts Dick and Jeri Bain, right, who enjoy re-creating the past.

The graceful interior of a fine house.

CHAMBERED NAUTILUS

A stately structure

The Chambered Nautilus is a classic colonial structure situated high on a hill in Seattle's university district. With elegant white columns flanking the entryway and supporting the graceful sun porch, the home is at once stately and gracious.

Both the first-floor living room and adjoining dining room, where innkeepers Deborah Sweet and Kate McDill serve breakfast, are equipped with working fireplaces. Breakfast might include homemade breads, waffles, fresh fruits, yogurt, or a savory quiche. One bite of Kate's buttery scones, rich coffee cakes, and feather-light muffins reveals her expertise as a baker.

Each of the large and airy bedrooms is furnished with thoughtfully coordinated beds and bureaus, and several rooms open onto private porches that overlook the ivy-covered hillside and colorful gardens. Throughout, contemporary graphic prints and delicate watercolors decorate the walls.

After breakfast, visitors may spend the day exploring the pleasures of Seattle and the sur-rounding area. Deborah is an avid runner who can guide guests to the best running paths in the neighborhood.

CHAMBERED NAUTILUS, 5005 22nd Avenue, N.E., Seattle, WA 98105; (206) 522-2536; Kate McDill and Deborah Sweet, hosts. Six rooms with three shared baths. Rates: $40 to $60. Includes plentiful continental breakfast of scones, muffins or coffee cake, fresh fruits and yogurts, and sometimes quiche or waffles. Children under twelve by special arrangement; no pets; smoking in living room only; Visa/MasterCard. The dog of the house, Keri, is a shy white Samoyed. Dinners, wine tastings, and other special events can be accommodated. The house is accessible only by a flight of steps.

DIRECTIONS: from I-5, take 50th St. East exit. Proceed about 1½ miles and turn left onto 20th Ave. N.E. Go four blocks and take a right onto 54th St. N.E. Proceed down a steep hill and turn right onto 22nd St. N.E.

THE SARATOGA INN

Sophisticated country comfort

Here Chippendale and Queen Anne furnishings mix with country pine and folk art. There is much warmth and whimsy in the décor, along with good taste and sophistication. At the Saratoga Inn the rooms look like pages from an interior design magazine, but they are wholly inviting.

Comfortable couches in the living room beckon you to curl up by the fire with a good book and a cup of tea or glass of wine. A dark blue carpet offsets a bright floral chair. Wooden decoys, a copper weather vane, and painted rocking horse harmonize with an Oriental rug and grandfather clock. A collection of lead soldiers belonging to innkeeper Ted Jones and his son are in a living room cabinet.

Upstairs, the bedrooms are beautifully appointed, with a distinguished collection of handmade quilts, early American antiques, monogrammed cotton sheets, and comfortable chairs.

On 25 acres overlooking the Saratoga Passage.

Picture windows offer stunning views of the quaint village of Langley, and large modern bathrooms are filled with a generous selection of sweet-smelling toiletries.

THE SARATOGA INN, 4850 South Coles Road, Langley, Whidbey Island, WA 98260; (206) 221-7526; Debbie and Ted Jones, hosts. Five guest rooms with private baths. Rates $55 to $75. Includes a delicious buffet breakfast. Children under fourteen by special arrangement only; no pets; smoking allowed on the outside porches only. Two cats and a golden retriever in residence. Within walking distance of Langley, a delightful seaside village with several fine shops, galleries, and an excellent theater.

DIRECTIONS: from Seattle, take I-5 north to Whidbey Island/ Mukilteo Ferry exit 189. Take the 15-minute ferry ride to Clinton on Whidbey Island. Proceed into Langley and take Third St., which becomes Brooks Hill Rd. Take a left onto Coles Rd. and the entrance to the inn is on the right.

The soft, cool colors were suggested by the handmade quilt on the wall.

Rustic choices

Situated on twenty-five acres of wooded property, Guest House offers several different styles of accommodations. Capturing the traditional flavor of a bed and breakfast inn, a one-story farmhouse contains two guest rooms, with antique furnishings, country quilts, shared bath, family-style dining room, and snug living room and fireplace. Behind that main farmhouse is a bright yellow one-room guest cottage, with a wide porch and knotty pine interior.

Bordering on a reflecting pond are the Carriage House, a sizable cabin in the woods with a skylight over the bed, and the Log Cabin, which is smaller and more rustic. Built of logs, it has a cozy sleeping loft, kitchen, and sitting area.

The most luxurious accommodation is the Lodge, a large two-story log home with a deck that reaches to the edge of the pond. Its appointments are classic: a massive stone fireplace, a moose head over the mantel, heavy wooden doors with iron latches.

GUEST HOUSE BED & BREAKFAST, 835 E. Christenson Road, Greenbank, Whidby Island, WA 98253; (206) 678-3115; Don and Mary Jane Creger, hosts. Three cottages and a lodge, all with private baths, kitchens, and fireplaces or wood stoves. Two guestrooms in the farmhouse with a shared bath. Rates: $30 to $85. Includes a full self-serve breakfast of cereals, muffins or croissant, and boiled eggs. No children under fourteen; no pets; no smoking; Visa/MasterCard.

DIRECTIONS: from Whidbey Island/Mukilteo Ferry, drive 16 miles on Rte. 525. At Christenson Rd. there are signs for "The Guest House." Proceed to driveway on left leading to yellow farmhouse.

The solarium, sun deck, and hot tub are discreetly tucked out of sight.

Formerly a farmhouse

Sally's Bed and Breakfast Manor is a snug and tidy farmhouse blessed with a wonderful view of the distant Cascade Mountains, the calm waters of the Saratoga Passage, and the tiny town of Langley.

The living room is decorated in soothing shades of sea green, soft colors that blend with the scenery and complement the handsome lines of the hearth. The two guest bedrooms are decorated in a harmonious blend of pastel fabrics, cozy comforters, and bright garden flowers. A tangy-sweet aroma of cinnamon pervades and scents the house, eliciting warm thoughts and comfortable memories.

Visitors are invited to stroll about the three acres of manicured grounds and amble through the raised-bed garden, where a profusion of grapes, berries, herbs, and vegetables thrive in this temperate climate. At Sally's, one and all are transported to a fair and pleasing world.

SALLY'S BED & BREAKFAST MANOR, 215 6th Street, P.O. Box 459, Langley, Whidbey Island, WA 98260; (206) 221-8709; Sally De Felice, owner. Two bedrooms with private *en suite* baths. Rates: $65. Includes full breakfast with egg dish, sausage, muffins, berries from the garden, and home-churned butter. No children; no pets; no smoking. Pumpkin is the cat in residence.

DIRECTIONS: take I-5 to the Whidbey Island/Mukilteo Ferry exit. Take the ferry to Clinton and proceed into Langley on Rte. 525. Turn right on Langley Road, pass the high school on the left and when you come to a Y in the road, take the left fork, which is 6th St.

CLIFF HOUSE

An architectural masterpiece

Designed to let in the light, this house captures the imagination.

Cliff House is simply breathtaking! Philip Johnson, the renowned architect who selected Cliff House to receive an AIA award in 1980, was particularly taken with the large open atrium rising through the center of the house and the profusion of natural light that floods the interior. As its name indicates, Cliff House sits on a bluff above the sea—its large windows revealing the drama of the Olympic Mountains in the distance, high above the Admiralty Straights. Ships steaming into Seattle pass offshore, and blood-red sunsets reflecting off the water, make this an unusually romantic and spectacularly beautiful place.

The interior of the house blends rugged stone with cedar structural beams, a luxurious sunken living room, plush carpeting, primitive art, delicate paintings, and nature photographs taken by the hostess, Peggy Moore. Because the house is so much a part of her life, Peggy is exhilarated by her guests' enthusiasm. She rents the one-bedroom house in its entirety, to one couple at a time.

CLIFF HOUSE, 5440 S. Grigware Road, Freeland, WA 98249; (206) 321-1566; Peggy Moore, hostess. The entire house is for rent. One bedroom with king-size bed with ocean view. Rates: $95. Includes continental breakfast. Cannot accommodate children or pets; non-smokers are preferred; no credit cards. Stairway to the beach and hot tub on outside deck in a 17-acre secluded wooded setting.

DIRECTIONS: from the Whidbey Island/Mukilteo Ferry, drive 11 miles on Rte. 525 and turn left onto Bush Point Rd. (after pizza parlor on left and Book Bay on right). Proceed 1¼ miles and turn left on Grigware Rd. The driveway is on the right.

The view of the sea from the king-sized bed is rapturous.

Dusk is a beautiful time at the farm.

THE MANOR FARM INN

A gentleman's farm

Grazing around the Manor Farm Inn's 1886 two-story white farmhouse are dozens of border Cheviot sheep, long-haired tan Highland cattle, and a herd of Guernsey cows. There are well-groomed horses in the barn and ducks around the pond, which was recently stocked with ten thousand rainbow trout. The twenty-five acres of rolling green meadows surrounding this century-old inn are punctuated by stark white wooden fences.

A rose-covered veranda leads from the parlor, past the guest rooms, and into the dining room. Hors d'oeuvres and sherry are served by the fire in the parlor, furnished with a good sampling of country pine antiques. The dining room's pine chairs were made in Appalachia. At tables covered with pink and white handwoven linens, a gourmet dinner is served by candlelight with classical music in the background. Roast quail, lobster, or flank steak in a plum-pear sauce can be one of the entrées in a five-course meal, and dinner is often completed with port and cheese three hours later.

The meals are prepared by host Robin Hughes, a former restaurateur. Robin believes that guests should encounter an entirely restorative experience here, consisting of elegant surroundings, enticing food, and exquisite serenity. A gentleman's farm, such as this, can provide these pleasures.

THE MANOR FARM INN, 26069 Big Valley Road, N.E., Poulsbo, WA 98110; (206) 779-4628; Robin and Jill Hughes, hosts. Ten guest rooms furnished with French country antiques, each with private bath and several with fireplaces. Rates: $50 to $75. Includes a continental breakfast brought to the room and lavish country breakfast in the dining room a bit later. Sherry and hors d'oeuvres served in the parlor. Hot tub available. No children; no pets; no smoking; Visa/MasterCard. Gourmet dinners with fixed price are served in the restaurant at one seating. Entire working farm open for guests' pleasure.

DIRECTIONS: from Seattle, take the Kingston Ferry and follow signs to Hood Canal Bridge. Just before the bridge take Rte. 3 south towards Lofall. Follow signs to Kitsap Memorial State Park and proceed until a large sign for Manor Farm Inn marks the turn onto Big Valley Road, NE.

CHANNEL HOUSE

Spectacular views of the San Juan Islands

From the large outdoor hot tub behind this house you can get a panoramic view of the sunset over Puget Sound and the boats navigating the Guemes Channel. Built in 1902, this three-story bungalow is just minutes from the ferry.

Furnished throughout with turn-of-the-century pieces, the guest rooms are large and airy and have antique brass, mahogany, and canopied beds. The main floor will make guests feel perfectly at home. There is a library and music room with its own fireplace, an inviting formal living room, and a tiled solarium filled with all manner of greenery. A full breakfast of fresh fruit, home-baked breads, and an assortment of egg dishes is served in the sunny dining room.

Host Sam Salzinger will offer an invitation, if the weather is good, to join him aboard his twenty-three-foot sailboat. But those who are partial to land can drive through nearby Washington Park to find a sandy beach and spectacular views of the San Juan Islands.

CHANNEL HOUSE, 2902 Oakes Avenue, Anacortes, WA 98221. (206) 293-9382. Sam and Kathy Salzinger, hosts. Four rooms with two shared baths. Rates: $40. Inquire about weekly rates. Includes a full breakfast of fruits, baked breads and egg dishes. No children under twelve; no pets. Smoking is permitted in the common areas but not in the rooms; no credit cards. Outdoor hot tub.

DIRECTIONS: from I-5, take Highway 20 west and follow signs to Anacortes Ferry, which will put you on Oakes Avenue. Follow the numbers to 2902 Oakes and Channel House is on the right.

Built by an Italian count in 1902.

Painting of the hostess at age seven with her grandfather.

KANGAROO HOUSE

Where quality of life matters

This bungalow-style house combines the romance of living on an island with the fruits of tradition. Brought from the mainland are the fine old cherrywood china closet that belonged to innkeeper Polly Nesbit's grandmother and the spindled four-poster bed that Polly slept in as a child.

Beautiful aspects of the island are in evidence too: the fieldstone fireplace that was built by the Nesbits with stones from a farmer's field.

Good restaurants, quaint shops, and galleries are to be found on Orcas Island, and there are swimming, fishing, and hiking at nearby Moran State Park.

KANGAROO HOUSE, P.O. Box 334, North Beach Road, Eastsound, Orcas Island, WA 98245; (206) 376-2175; Ken and Polly Nesbit, hosts. Five guest rooms with shared baths. Four with sinks in the room. Rates: $40 to $55. Includes a full breakfast of baked eggs, fresh fruits, and baked breads. Children under twelve by previous arrangement; no pets; smoking permitted in living room only; Visa/MasterCard. Check during January and February as to exact dates of winter closing schedule.

DIRECTIONS: the island can be reached by air from Seattle or via the Washington State Ferry, which has seven departures each day from Anacortes and takes about 1¼ hrs. Once on Orcas follow the ferry traffic and the signs into Eastsound. Take a left at the only traffic light onto North Beach Rd. and go about a mile. The house is on the left.

OVERLEAF: *Washington State Ferry arriving at picturesque Orcas Island.*

STARRETT HOUSE INN

Majestic purple mansion

This is an extraordinary Victorian inn, with an exterior and interior that are architecturally fascinating. George Starrett was an architect and contractor who built more than three hundred and fifty homes. Because Port Townsend was being considered as the state capital, Starrett anticipated a great deal of future building and created this house as his showcase. He took seven years to build his masterpiece, which is four stories high and a combination of five different Victorian styles: Carpenter Gothic, Gay Carpenter, Queen Anne, Stick, and Eastlake.

Perhaps the most spectacular feature of the home is a three-story sweeping spiral staircase culminating in an exquisite painted dome that opulently depicts the four seasons. At the time of the winter and summer solstices, rays of light entering narrow windows of the tower shine directly into the exact center of the dome.

The two front parlors house a fine restaurant, where breakfast is served on white linen tablecloths with elegant silver. Continental cuisine for dinner, including crêpes de la mer, chicken Denison, tender steaks, and marvelous desserts, are all prepared under the supervision of innkeeper and chef Susan Thompson. Guests are often invited into a third parlor for after-dinner coffee or a cordial by the fire.

The house is filled with lovely, carefully selected antiques that are in keeping with its grandeur. One feels in staying here the sense of having briefly encountered the glamour of another era.

STARRETT HOUSE INN & RESTAURANT, 744 Clay Street, Port Townsend, WA 98368; (206) 385-2976; Mack and Susan Thompson, hosts. Nine rooms with shared baths. Rates: $50 to $75. Includes coffee or tea delivered on silver service to the bedroom and a delicious breakfast of bountiful proportions in the dining room. Children under twelve by special arrangement; no pets; Visa/MasterCard. Fanny, a grey cat, and Samuel, an old English sheep dog, in residence. Public house tours given daily, 12–4 PM. Restaurant open Friday through Monday, 5–10 PM.

DIRECTIONS: from the Port Townsend Ferry Dock, proceed into downtown area and make a left onto Quincy St. In two blocks turn right onto Adams and continue to Clay.

Looking down from the spiral staircase (pictured opposite the title page), one glimpses the dining rooms and parlor.

Left, a charming bedroom captures the flavor of another era, as does the beautifully restored house, above.

HASTINGS HOUSE INN

Tower views of Port Townsend

Carefully maintained as a family residence until it became an inn, Hastings House never required restoration, and today it is on the National Register of Historic Landmarks. Built in 1889 by one of the founders of Port Townsend, Frank Hasting's home can be described as a Queen Anne Victorian with an Edwardian influence.

Two elegant turrets, a wraparound porch, a quarter-turn staircase, Italian ceramic fireplaces, hand-rubbed oak woodwork, and an Italian blown glass grape chandelier are original to the house. The old furniture is no longer here, but the house has been decorated with a sensitivity to the period and to its architectural lines and scale. Everything is simple and elegant and looks as if it belongs.

Rising three stories, the turret at the front corner of the house creates delightful circular alcoves in the main floor parlor and in the master and third-floor bedrooms. Each of the upstairs alcoves serves as a charming sitting room for the bedrooms, and each has a marvelous view of Admiralty Inlet.

Bruce and Grace Peirson, who manage this inn, say they "try to keep guests happy and comfortable." Happiness and comfort are just what you'll find.

HASTINGS HOUSE INN, Washington and Walker Streets, Port Townsend, WA 98368; (206) 385-3553; Bruce and Grace Peirson, managers. Seven rooms, private and shared baths. Rates: $45 to $75. Winter rates slightly less. Includes continental breakfast of fruit, cinnamon rolls, bread pudding, and cereals. Children under twelve by arrangement; no pets; no smoking; Visa/MasterCard.

DIRECTIONS: from Seattle take the ferry to Winslow and follow the signs to Hood Canal Bridge. Cross bridge and follow signs to Port Townsend. After the first set of lights turn left onto Washington St. Go one block to the top of the hill and the house is on the corner.

A tower guest room.

LIZZIE'S

It is easy to feel at home

Formerly head of a construction company that did nothing but restoration, Thelma Scudi purchased this place in ten minutes flat. Coming upon it on a day off from her job, she had no intention of buying or opening an inn. "No one was more surprised than I," she says.

Four years after that fateful day, Lizzie's—named after Lizzie Grant, the colorful widow of a Port Townsend sea captain—shines with glistening new paint, plumbing, wiring, sprinklers, bathrooms, and kitchen. The Italianate Victorian building is admirably furnished with Queen Anne chairs, a Victorian leather chesterfield sofa, a brilliant red carpet, and a Knabe grand piano. Silk hangings from the Broadway production of *The Flower Drum Song* hang on either side of a marble fireplace. The inn is not pretentious, and it is easy to feel at home here.

This 1880s Italianate Victorian is part of Port Townsend's legacy. Right, the Federal lighthouse at Fort Warden, near Port Townsend.

Breakfasts are served at a twelve-foot oak table in the kitchen, amid welcome informality. Cast-iron muffin tins, a Chinese bamboo steamer, a wire egg basket, and other cooking utensils hang from a handmade iron pot rack overhead. There is a big old hotel stove with six burners, two ovens, and three broilers that is used to serve up a generous continental breakfast of gingerbread, scones, and coffee cake.

Thelma Scudi also markets her own brand of Lizzie's toiletries. The custom-made apricot soaps and lotions are her trademark. There is a sense of merriment and gaiety here, generated by the hostess' quick sense of humor. Lizzie's is fun.

Tasteful Victorian furnishings make Charlie's Room a favorite.

LIZZIE'S, 731 Pierce Street, Port Townsend, WA 98368; (206) 385-4168; Thelma Scudi, owner. Seven rooms tastefully decorated, private and shared baths. Rates: $42 to $79. Includes generous continental breakfast of fresh breads such as gingerbread, scones or coffeecake, and fruits. Children over twelve; no pets; smoking permitted, but no pipes or cigars in bedrooms; Visa/MasterCard. Brenda, a Staffordshire terrier, is in residence. Check during Nov. to Feb. for winter closing schedule. Lizzie's brand of soaps and lotions available for purchase.

DIRECTIONS: from the Port Townsend Ferry take a right onto Water St., in one block take a left onto Taylor St. At the fountain, turn left onto Washington St. Proceed up the hill and turn right at the post office onto Pierce and proceed six blocks. From the south, at the third Port Townsend stoplight take a left onto Taylor St. and proceed as above.

BED & BREAKFAST RESERVATION AGENCIES

The concept of Bed and Breakfast in the United States is rapidly expanding. To facilitate this phenomenon, reservation agencies are quickly cropping up, resulting in rapidly changing information. Many of the agencies listed below have been in existence for some time; others have been organized recently. Do not be surprised if there are changes when you contact them.

California

AMERICAN FAMILY INN/BED AND BREAKFAST SAN FRANCISCO, P.O. Box 349, San Francisco, CA 94101; (415) 931-3083; Richard and Susan Kreibich. Call any time. Private residences and luxurious yachts. San Francisco, Marin County, Carmel/Monterey, the Wine Country, and Lake Tahoe.

AMERICAN HISTORIC HOMES BED & BREAKFAST, P.O. Box 336, Dana Point, CA 92629; (714) 496-7050; Deborah Sakach. 9 A.M. to 5 P.M. National landmarks, plantations, seaside cottages, and Queen Anne cottages. California, including Los Angeles and San Francisco; New York City, Boston, and Washington, D.C.

BED AND BREAKFAST EXCHANGE, P.O. Box 88, St. Helena, CA 94574; (707) 963-7756; Andee Beresini. Vacation homes. Wine Country.

BED AND BREAKFAST INTERNATIONAL, 151 Ardmore Road, Kensington, CA 94707; (415) 527-8836 or 525-4569; Jean Brown. 8 A.M. to 5:30 P.M. weekdays; 9 A.M. to noon on Saturdays. Private homes, apartments, houseboats, penthouses. California, Hawaii, Seattle, Las Vegas, Chicago, Boston, New York City, and Washington, D.C.

BED AND BREAKFAST OF LOS ANGELES, 32127 Harborview Lane, Westlake Village, CA 91361; (213) 889-7325—Peg Marshall. (213) 889-8870—Angie Kobabe. From Ventura to San Clemente.

BED AND BREAKFAST RENT-A-ROOM INTERNATIONAL, 11531 Varna Street, Garden Grove, CA 92640; (714) 638-1406; Esther H. MacLachlan. Private homes. Los Angeles to San Diego and Palm Desert.

CALIFORNIA HOUSEGUESTS INTERNATIONAL, 6051 Lindley Avenue, #6, Tarzana, CA 91356; (213) 344-7878; Trudi Alexy. Apartments, and mansions with ocean views. Greater Los Angeles, Santa Monica, Malibu, Santa Barbara, Carmel/Monterey, San Francisco, San Diego, etc.

CAROLYN'S BED & BREAKFAST HOMES, P.O. Box 84776, San Diego, CA 92138; (619) 481-7662; Carolyn Waskiewicz. 8 A.M. to 7 P.M. San Diego.

CHRISTIAN BED AND BREAKFAST OF AMERICA, P.O. Box 388, San Juan Capistrano, CA 92693; (714) 496-7050; Sue Duggan. 9 A.M. to 5 P.M. Homes in 200 cities including Palm Springs, Anchorage, Washington, D.C.

CO-HOST BED & AMERICAN BREAKFAST, 11715 S. Circle Drive, Whittier, CA 90601; (213) 699-8427; Coleen Davis. 8 A.M. to 9 P.M. Mountain, beach, and in-town residences. Covers the whole of California.

EYE OPENERS BED & BREAKFAST RESERVATIONS, Box 694, Altadena, CA 91001; 213-684-4428 or 797-2055. Ruth Judkins and Elizabeth Cox. 9 A.M. to 6 P.M. Private homes and historic houses. Los Angeles County.

BED AND BREAKFAST HOMESTAY, P.O. Box 326, Cambria, CA 93428; 805-927-4613; Alex Laputz. Call any time. Ocean views and secluded custom built homes. Hearst Castle area and California central coastal region.

HOME SUITE HOMES, 1470 Firebird Way, Sunnyvale, CA 94087; (408) 733-7215; Rhonda Robins. International listings—United States, England, France, Spain, and Mexico.

NAPA VALLEY BED & BREAKFAST, 1910 First Street, Napa, CA 94559; (707) 257-1051; Jim and Carol Beazley; Carol Knight. Victorian homes and farm houses. Napa Valley.

SEAVIEW RESERVATIONS BED & BREAKFAST, P.O. Box 1355, Laguna Beach, CA 92652; (714) 494-8878; Nancy Fine and Marcia Mordkin. Full range of private homes. Laguna Beach and other prime areas along or near the California coast.

Oregon

GRISWOLD BED & BREAKFAST AGENCY, 552 West Broadway, Eugene, OR 97401; (503) 683-6294; Phyllis Griswold. Log cabin, resort, manor, restored and modern homes. Leaburg, Elmira, Coburg, and Eugene.

NORTHWEST BED AND BREAKFAST, 7707 S.W. Locust Street, Portland, OR 97223; (503) 246-8366; Laine Friedman and Gloria Shaich. 8 A.M. to 5 P.M. weekdays. 9 A.M. to 1 P.M. Saturday. Farms, ranches, Victorian, contemporary, mountain, and ocean front homes. International listings. Coverage extends throughout the United States and Canada. Includes Bed and Breakfast tours of Great Britain.

Washington

PACIFIC BED & BREAKFAST, 701 N.W. 60th Street, Seattle, WA 98107; (206) 784-0539; Irmgard Castleberry. 7 A.M. to 7 P.M. weekdays. Mansions, Victorians, a houseboat, island cottages, and contemporary lakefront homes. Covers Pacific Northwest.

RSVP BED & BREAKFAST RESERVATION SERVICE, P.O. Box 778, Ferndale, WA 98248; (206) 384-6586; Linda Jolly. 9 A.M. to 1 P.M. daily. Island, turn-of-the-century, modest, and honeymoon-quality homes for families and for the handicapped. Covers Skagit, Snohomish, Whatcom and Island counties to Canadian border and Vancouver, British Columbia.

TRAVELLERS' BED & BREAKFAST, P.O. Box 492, Mercer Island, WA 98040; (206) 232-2345; Jean Knight. 8 A.M. to 5:30 P.M. daily. Apartments, houseboats, and waterfront homes. Over 70 accommodations in Seattle and Vancouver, British Columbia.